THE WORLD OF
THE
HORSE

THE WORLD OF
THE
HORSE

URSULA BRUNS
ELISABETH WEILAND

OCTOPUS BOOKS

Contents

A Ridgmount book

First published 1986 by Octopus Books Ltd
59 Grosvenor Street, London W1

© 1976 Albert Müller Verlag, AG, Rüschlikon-Zürich

© 1986 English translation Ridgmount Books Ltd

ISBN 0 7064 2689 4

Translated, adapted and designed by John Youé & Associates

Produced by Mandarin Publishers Ltd
22a Westlands Road
Quarry Bay, Hong Kong

Printed in Hong Kong

Foreword

Writer Ursula Bruns, and photographer Elisabeth Weiland, have combined their talents and drawn on their immense international experience to create this book. Inevitably most of the interest and action is centred on the Westernized countries of the world – but not exclusively. For example there are fascinating accounts of unusual working and sporting equestrian events in faraway places such as Japan, the Cameroons, Mongolia and India.

Nearer to home, the authors describe the exhilarating lives of horses in the wild; the first year of life is sensitively captured in words and photographs; and the history of many forms of riding and equestrian events – and of the breeds and how they were specially developed for each purpose – is knowledgeably presented.

Bruns and Weiland highlight many aspects of the simple yet gratifying pleasures that amateur riders can enjoy; and of course they cover the colourful and thrilling spectacle of major sporting events such as the Olympics, international trials and show-jumping.

The relationship – and in many instances the interdependence – between horse and man has existed for centuries. This book captures and projects the rich pleasure and satisfaction we all can enjoy by a more complete understanding of the world of the horse.

THE EDITOR

Introduction:
THE MAGIC OF THE HORSE

Horses are magical creatures, and can instil some of their magic into our lives. If we ride, and if we allow horses to play a part in our everyday existence, then we know that we are among life's lucky ones. Horses are filled with the joy of living – dash, energy and independent self-reliance – and they communicate some of this vital, primitive power to us. Surely this is magic of a sort.

In this book we shall explore the world of the horse by travelling all over the Earth, from China to South America, from Canada and the United States to Africa and Europe. We shall look at horses of all types: the Mongolian horse and the Quarter-horse, the Shetland Pony and the Arab, the horse in the Olympic dressage competition and the horse that works for its living in the world's wilder parts. And we shall look at the riders, too: nomads and cowboys, jockeys and farmers, sporting competitors and, of course, the untold millions of people who ride horses simply for the fun of it.

It is easy to forget that, not so long ago, many breeds of horse seemed to be facing extinction. First the steam engine and then, much more significantly, the internal-combustion engine took over many of the horse's traditional roles. The new machines were noisier and smellier, and could hardly be regarded as a friend in the way that a horse can be . . . but they were generally more efficient and, importantly, cheaper to run. It looked as if working horses would disappear altogether, leaving only the horses used in racing, the pets of a few very rich people, and the ever-decreasing numbers of animals in the world's few remaining herds of wild horses.

But then everything changed and the horse came into its own again. People who had previously had nothing to do with them became interested. All over the Western hemisphere more foals were bred and more horses were bought and sold. To be sure, the demand now was for horses which were lighter, smaller and consequently more lively than before, but the situation represented an abrupt turnaround

nevertheless. What had happened was that people had started, more and more, to want horses not for pulling their carts or carrying them into battle but to share their leisure hours. The great era of riding for pleasure had begun.

An Adaptable Friend
The horse is an animal which can be used to pull and to carry. So, of course, can the camel, the donkey, the mule, the ox and many others; but on aggregate the horse displays outstanding advantages over the rest. It is much fleeter of foot than all (except, on rare occasions, the camel); and it is one of the most intelligent of all our domesticated animals. But perhaps its greatest single advantage lies in its adaptability.

Horses can survive almost anywhere in the world if left to fend for themselves: they can cope with changes in both climate and fodder. They can stand the Arctic cold of Siberia and the hot moist sultriness of Indonesia, as well as the great deserts of Sudan and Arabia, the Gobi and Australia. You find the horse among the winds and crackling frosts of the Russian steppes and the rugged inhospitability of Tierra del Fuego; there are horses working thousands of feet above sea-level in the frozen Andes and deep beneath the surface of the Earth in some of the world's mines. Not only can horses endure extremes of temperature, they can tolerate extreme temperature *changes* as well, from subzero cold at midnight to the sweltering heat of the midday sun. They seem equally unconcerned by the snowstorms of the Arctic wastes and the sand-storms of the Sahara.

Similarly, the horse is astonishingly flexible in terms of fodder. Dry grass, fresh grass, even saline grass – all seem equally acceptable. It will dig into the earth to eat roots or through a thick

An Arab stallion, pride of the Cameroon National Stud, rears in an impressive display of strength.

layer of snow to munch whatever it may find. Twigs from bushes and young trees, bark, straw, the bitter and prickly plants of the steppes, your great-aunt's straw hat, the sharp reeds of the salt lakes of the Camargue – all these and more will be contentedly processed by the horse's remarkable digestive system.

There is another and far less generally appreciated aspect of the horse's adaptability, namely that the animal is capable of adjusting its body size according to the prevailing circumstances. Of course, this is adaptation working at generation level rather than effecting changes in the individual, but it is significant nonetheless. Essentially, good food and a benign climate lead to bigger horses, while generally adverse conditions of climate – either too hot or too cold – and a subsistence diet will engender smaller animals, right down to the pigmy-like Shetland Pony, the smallest native horse (although the strongest for its size) in the British Isles, superbly adapted to the winds, rain and treelessness of Shetland.

While there is no 'right' size for a horse, most horses leading a near-to-natural existence stand about 12 to 14 hands tall. About two-thirds of the world's horses are in this size-range, including the horses of Iceland, Ireland, the moors of southern Britain, the mountains of Scandinavia, Austria and the Balkans, and the plains of Eastern Europe. Where mankind has interceded in the horse's development, either through deliberate breeding or simply by protecting the horse from the full rigours of nature, individual animals tend to be larger. For example, in the United States the Quarter-horses and the Morgans are generally a little over 15 hands tall, and the same is true of the Paso Finos of Latin America.

Thus the horse is remarkably sensitive to its environment, which means that the genus *Equus* is very swift to change and adapt. Only 50 million years ago (not long, in evolutionary terms), during the Eocene Epoch, the horse was an animal about the size of a terrier. It lived in North America, the main centre of horse evolution. At various stages, when the geography and climate permitted, horses migrated from there to all the other continents of the world except Australia and Antarctica. Its legs grew longer, to allow greater speed, and the two bones of the lower limb fused into one, thereby minimizing the chances of twisting and consequent sprains. The feet grew smaller and simpler, improving the animal's running abilities; the toes on either side of the foot disappeared, so that most of the body-weight was concentrated on the middle toe; and by about 25 million years ago the horse was, in essence, a single-toed animal. Throughout this time it was growing bigger, but interestingly it remained a very light animal in terms of its size;

once again, this was an adaptation to improve its running. Indeed, although it is not the fastest creature over short distances, there is no animal in the world better adapted for running than the modern race-horse.

The evolutionary history of the horse is a fascinating one and we know it in better detail than for any other animal, with the possible exception of man, thanks to the remarkable fossil sequences found in the United States and investigated by, notably, Othniel Charles Marsh and Edward Drinker Cope in the nineteenth century. In fact, the horse's evolutionary history was mapped out so precisely because of fierce competition and bitter rivalry between these two palaeontologists. Both were tough and determined men. Marsh was guided all over the western United States by none other than Buffalo Bill Cody. Cope covered much the same territory and the story goes that, on one occasion, he saved himself from death at the hands of Red Indians only by using his false teeth. The Indians' hostility waned as they watched in amazement while Cope popped his teeth repeatedly into and out of his mouth!

The sensitivity of the horse's evolutionary response is largely a result of the animal's fecundity; and, when this is taken in tandem with the ability of the various different types of horse to interbreed, mankind is presented with a powerful means of creating exactly the type of horse desired for various different purposes. The muscular pack-horse, the colossus of the knight in armour, the light speedy runner of the race-track and the sinewy Arab for fighting in the desert – all have been a product of the horse's natural powers of adaptation in conjunction with the intervention of mankind.

In terms of behaviour, too, man has had a profound impact on the horse. By nature horses are gentle herbivores whose instinct at any sign of trouble is to turn and flee. Yet, on instructions from human beings, horses will with apparent willingness jump over hedges and across streams, run dangerously close to milling cattle, pursue vicious animals like boars and lions in the hunt, and even, in days gone by, enter the turmoil of battle amid the thunder of cannonfire. Even today, in some luckless parts of the world, horses are used as fighting-vehicles.

Peace and War

Despite their gentleness, though, horses can on occasion be dangerous. They are easily frightened, and when this happens their reactions can be violent. They are bigger than a man, quicker and stronger. They can bite, kick, strike and bolt – especially if mishandled. Certainly part of the fascination of horses is that they are potentially such wild creatures. However placid and obedient a horse might be, you are always conscious of its underlying power. This duality of attraction is well captured by an ancient scribe, who wrote of Alexander the Great's horse, Bucephalos (meaning 'bull-headed'), that *the large eyes, full and clear, look out with such fidelity, such purity, such goodness: they radiate the fiery clarity of proud courage*. But we have to remember that, however powerful the horse may be, it is not by nature a bellicose beast. Any warlike characteristics which we ascribe to it are really products of our own imaginations, not inherent traits of the animal itself.

There are two main reasons for our error of understanding: firstly, that the horse is an extremely obedient animal; and secondly that its mannerisms can *look* far more wild, arrogant and violent than in fact they are. The horse paws the ground impatiently, kicks out with its hindlegs and strikes out with its forelegs, tosses its mane, flicks its tail . . . all of which looks splendidly martial to the observer but in fact has nothing at all to do with underlying aggression.

There is perhaps another reason – one which has nothing to do with the character or behaviour of the horse itself but a lot to do with the nature of its rider. For a man on the back of a horse is not just physically elevated: from his lofty vantage-point he tends to feel spiritually superior to his lower and slower-moving fellows. The better he can ride the horse, the greater his pride and self-confidence. There is nothing *wrong* with such pride – usually. In some people, however, what may be bred in the rider is not healthy pride but arrogance. Moreover, centuries ago, the civilizations with horses were the ones which overran and subjugated the peoples who were without them – again a cause for arrogance. It is hardly surprising that this arrogance of the rider was attributed also to the horse, and so the belief that the horse was a martial animal was strengthened.

Once again there was magic at work in mankind's relationship with the horse, but this time it was bad magic – magic which led to the wholesale slaughter of millions of terrified horses on the fields of war.

Good Magic

But there is good magic at work in the partnership as well – as anyone who has ever been in contact with a horse will know. The eye is captivated by the sight of this noble beast, and the imagination sparked by its grace and power.

The horse has an uncommonly pleasant *feel* when you touch it. Its body-hairs are fine and soft – especially on the head – and they press themselves smoothly and evenly to the shape of the body. The mouth is as soft as silk. The nostrils flutter gently under the touch of a hand, while the muscles stand out firmly yet sleekly on the neck and quarters. The long hair of the mane and tail can be thick and dense, tumbling down exuberantly, or it can be thin, spare and shining – both are equally appealing to the hand and eye.

And the horse comes in many colours. The coat and long hairs can be black, chestnut, golden, grey, white or any shade of yellow or brown. Often the body-hair and the long hair are of different colours: a golden Palomino can bear a white mane and tail, and there are countless other combinations. Some horses have coats in dappled patterns of two or more colours, while there are others whose coats are a single colour but whose manes are patterned in three. Some horses are speckled with dots, while some have coats of different colours for summer and winter. All these visual feasts have their particular admirers.

Another point is that the horse is the most pleasant animal of all to ride: just ask somebody who has ridden a camel, for example! Whatever the style of movement the horse is asked to make, it seems in some strange way to be tailor-made for the comfort of the rider. Of course, this is to a great extent the result of the rider learning to move with the horse; but it is also a product of the part that mankind has played in the modern evolution of the horse, not to mention a reasonable admixture of good fortune. Whatever the truth of the matter, there can be no denying the fact that riding a horse can often be a deeply satisfying experience – whether you are ambling along slowly on a leisurely evening ride at the end of a hot summer's day or galloping across fields and leaping over hedges and streams.

All of these things are magic, perhaps, but there is still something more – an extra 'something' which more than any other aspect of the horse's partnership with mankind brings the word 'magic' to one's lips.

Looking after a child – providing food and comfort and reassurance – brings out the best in most people, and the same is true when it is a horse rather than a child which is being looked after. Over the millennia, as mankind has taken the horse further and further from nature, the 'looking after' has increased in importance. People have had to learn to understand the horse in order to care for it better – not necessarily for altruistic reasons, as we have seen. But the more that mankind has had to understand the horse, the more time and attention that have had to be devoted to the horse's care and upkeep, the deeper has grown the bond of affection that maintains mankind's unique partnership with the horse. Our relations with the horse, in other words, have made us better people.

Which is inarguably magic at work . . . and *good* magic!

HORSES IN THE WILD

When you look at a herd of wild horses, you are looking back into time.

On the island of Gotland, in the Baltic to the southeast of Sweden, lives a very old race of horses. Recent fossil finds show that these Gotland-Russ ponies – which are usually about 12 hands tall and brown in colour – have lived on the island since at least the third millennium BC. They may have migrated there in the wake of the retreating glaciers at the end of the last glacial period of the Pleistocene (current) Ice Age. Even longer is the history of the Exmoor Pony. Perhaps a little smaller than the Gotland-Russ, these dark brown ponies are known from recent fossil researches to have survived without detectable change for a million years or more. It may be that the Exmoor Pony is a descendant of the Alaska Pony, since both share the same jaw structure.

Wild horses are, as you might expect, superbly adapted to their environments. In the West German industrial heartland, where the winters are severe, you can find horses to whom the cold means nothing. Their ancestors lived for thousands of years in the ice-cold steppes and mountain regions of Asia, where not only are winter temperatures amazingly low but there are hardly any trees or bushes to give protection from the frigid blasts of wind. Today, their winter coats give these horses an excellent defence from the cold: very fine hairs curl thickly close to the skin, and are covered by longer, coarser hairs. Snow is unable to penetrate to the skin, and eventually drops off as it is melted by the animal's body-heat.

At the other end of the scale are the horses of southern France, which are primarily adapted to withstand the hot summers of the Camargue; but even these horses can withstand the cold well – and Mediterranean winters can be very raw. Lakes and ponds freeze so hard that horses can walk on them, and have to beat with their hooves to break a hole through the ice in order to find drinking water. It is fascinating, too, to watch the Camargue horses as they scrape out the scarce food from under the snow. They drop their heads slowly and cautiously, puff out the warm air from their nostrils to melt a hole, and then feel delicately with their frost-covered lips for a blade of grass or the leaf of a plant.

The Herd

Herding is the key to the survival of horses in the wild. In herds they can survive the extremes of weather easily. And the herd is more than just a haphazard collection of animals; it is their home, and they know their place in it.

Horses which have escaped from captivity form herds as readily as do wild ones. The herd of wild horses now to be found in Westphalia is made up of the descendants of those that became separated from their owners there during the Thirty Years' War. In South America, a handful of Spanish horses escaped during the battle for what later became Buenos Aires. They formed groups which were so successful that a chronicler of the time recorded with amazement, only 50 years later, that herds of up to 20,000 animals had been reported. In both cases, an interesting point is that the original horses had come from numerous different races. When horses are forming the core of a new herd like this it doesn't matter how much of a hodge-podge of different breeds the original founding fathers represent.

Unlike any other animal closely involved with mankind, the horse, as soon as it returns from domestication to join a herd, forgets all the habits it has learned during its association with people. In some respects this is a good thing, but it can mean that many highly bred, highly sensitive horses, descendants of generations of animals which have enjoyed all the luxuries of captivity, experience hard times as they adapt to the wild.

Native German ponies from Westphalia patiently await the coming of the spring, seeking what shelter they can from the icy winter winds. They are excellently adapted to face both heat and cold.

The individuals may be handicapped by comparison with their wilder fellows, and it may be some generations before their offspring develop thicker coats and stronger teeth with which to cope with winter's rough dietary regime of brushwood and branches. The mares may give birth to smaller, less sturdy foals. Nevertheless, each new succeeding generation will be tougher, more resilient and more robust. And, despite what are quite literally initial teething troubles when horses return to the wild, it is worth stressing just how successfully they can do so, and with how little real difficulty. Apart from a few exceptions, even horses which have lived totally isolated from nature and from their fellows soon adapt to this new mode of existence, and in no time at all pick up the whole range of characteristic movements and noises required for life within the social framework of the herd.

As, of course, they must: horses are vulnerable in many different ways, they eat slowly, and they can defend themselves from predators only by flight. A solitary horse would have little chance of surviving, because it would either have to take so much time being on the alert for predators that it would have difficulty eating or, if it settled for long leisurely meals, it would inevitably become a meal itself.

In the herd, by contrast, responsibilities are divided among numerous different animals. While some of the horses are feeding, others keep their eyes and ears open for any sign of danger. If you study a herd of horses in the wild you will notice that some of the mares are standing still, as if bored, looking idly around with what seems to be lazy indifference. It isn't, of course. Nothing much may be happening, but they are ready to warn the herd of the slightest sign of any impending threat. From time to time you will see one or other of these drop her head to the ground to graze; simultaneously a different mare will shake herself a little, move a few steps to one side, and take over the watch.

Safety is important but so too is adequate food, and it is one of the duties of the herd's principal mare to smell out food and lead the others to it. Once again, if you study a wild herd closely over a long period you will notice a curious thing: different feeding-places are preferred at different times of the day. After a period of general dozing or sleeping, one mare will always begin to walk off in a definite direction and the others will follow her lead without any argument. She

knows which food tastes best at that time of the day and where it is to be found.

In order to function well, with each member aware of its responsibilities, a herd needs a strict hierarchy with every individual having a set place within the organizational structure. Status within this hierarchy is established by fighting for rank. A stallion may make it clear from the outset that he is the horse in charge, but most modern herds are run by a mare (the leading mare). It all depends which horse in the group can permanently achieve superiority over all the others. It's interesting to note that this in no way means that the biggest, fieriest horse is the leader – in fact, it is far more usually a phlegmatic one or even an undersized but lively mare. This may seem paradoxical, but only because of our tendency to graft human characteristics onto horses: that pacing, snorting beautiful beast is in fact displaying many of the signs of nervousness. The phlegmatic, apparently rather stupid one is in reality much more self-confident; while the undersized horse has had to struggle for its share of fodder since birth and has therefore developed a strong will and a general, overall toughness. Either of them may be capable of banishing that 'fiery' animal to a distant, if temporary, refuge with no more than a flick of the ears.

The most heated clashes between herd-members are for the dominant position at the top. The smallest weakness displayed by a leading mare will cause a younger one instinctively to attack her. Initially these attacks will probably be warded off successfully, but any further signs of weakness will inevitably lead to the leading mare's downfall. Nature, after all, will not tolerate weakness: a poor leader endangers the entire herd. For a horse to stay at the top it must have plenty of strength and energy – for the good of all.

With the leadership established the other ranking positions are also fought for, but often these skirmishes are nothing more than minor squabbles. The weaker horses know that they have no chance against the stronger ones and so, after a minimal display of token aggression, settle down placidly in their inferior status. Of course, these ranking positions are not permanent: whenever a new horse joins the group, the hierarchy is disrupted and a fresh round of squabbling and fighting must take place in order that a new structure can be established. Similarly, although new foals in a firmly bonded herd will take their mother's rank at birth, even the yearlings, as they play, are already putting each other to the test, to see which of them can get its own way for the longest time.

To the human eye these contests over status may seem to be a waste of time, but in fact each

As with many horses of that colour, the foals of the famous wild white horses of the Camargue in the South of France are born dark-brown and become lighter and lighter as they mature.

These brown Gotland-Russ ponies are survivors of the second most ancient extant breed in the world, the only older one being the Exmoor from the Southwest of England.

member of the herd can feel secure only if it knows its exact place within the organization: it must understand its own responsibilities towards the horses of lower caste, and also that the stronger animals in the herd are there to protect it. The defeated leading mare takes up her new, lower-ranking position without any resentment; her waning powers have brought her release from the responsibilities of leadership. The new principal mare may not display much by way of consideration for the feelings of others, but nor does she spend her time making overt displays of her dominance in the way that leaders of groups of anthropoid apes do. She simply accepts her new-found dominance, as do the other members of the herd . . . until, in turn, she begins to show signs of weakness.

These are ancient instincts, and thousands of years of domestication have not succeeded in extinguishing them. Every horse will unquestioningly obey one of higher rank. In fact, it is probably for exactly this reason that people are able to ride, drive, load or otherwise bend horses to their will. After the initial fight to tame a horse, it is man which provides it with protection and fodder; in other words, we are fulfilling the role of a higher-ranking horse, and so the animal is prepared to accept us as such without argument. Among domesticated horses themselves there are still established ranks – as anyone involved with a

group of horses will tell you.

Horses like to graze in scattered groups, not too close to each other but close enough to come together quickly at the first sign of danger. In large parts of the modern world, of course, few threats to such herds persist, but nevertheless the horses still possess their primeval, instinctive fears. Strange people can frighten them, as can unaccustomed noises, and in moments the herd will group together behind the principal mare – preferably lined up in single file behind her, following in her tracks. Until they are satisfied that all is well they will stick to safe areas; then, once the leading mare has shown that the coast is clear, all the horses will spread out again and continue grazing. Although the scene is tranquil, however, the mares will still be sharing sentry duty as before, alert for the next sign of danger that may appear.

As always in the wild, peace and calm are relative things.

Mating Behaviour

After safety and fodder, the third most important thing in the herd's life is procreation. It should be stressed, though, that procreation is very definitely subordinate to the other two: the full mating urge asserts itself only when the twin prerequisites of a secure existence and a regular and adequate food supply are established. In these ideal conditions the herd will multiply with astonishing speed; but when the circumstances are less than ideal a significantly smaller number of foals will be born.

Mating has a dominant influence on the behaviour of the stallions. The leading mare need not be by any means the best in the herd when it comes to the task of foal-bearing, but the leading stallion will always be the most sexually productive: this may be because the strength of his sexual urges forces him to achieve physical superiority over the other stallions in the herd, or it may be the other way around, that the strong sex urge is a consequence of the physical potency. The intricacies of sex are as mysterious among horses as they are among humans.

Icelandic ponies were brought to the island by the first settlers a thousand years ago. For centuries they were the only means of transport in Iceland.

Certainly, though, there is a large psychological factor at work in the stallion's sexual behaviour. It has long been observed that, after a fight between stallions, the loser stops showing any desire to cover the mares, and this lack of interest may last quite a while. Presumably the shock of defeat quenches the urge to mate. Moreover, if the principal stallion is extremely strong, and is able to defend his exclusive use of several mares, the young stallions may join together with the old, defeated stallions to form bachelor herds. In fact this is inevitable, for male and female foals are born in roughly equal numbers and the strong stallions will always be able to claim several mares for themselves. All-male herds obviously cannot produce new members to replace the old through procreation, but they may nevertheless be reasonably stable, long-lasting groups as new recruits arrive in the form of 'surplus' stallions from the main herd. (Gelding eliminates this sort of problem in domesticated groups.)

It would be a mistake to assume that the fights between stallions need necessarily produce a clear winner or a clear loser. Often enough a compromise position is achieved. Hans W. Silvester has described this at some length:

The herd grazes contentedly. The foals play and, as usual, the stallion grazes a little to one side of the rest. Suddenly he raises his head, flares his nostrils and breathes deeply. He gives a loud neigh and the foals flee to their mothers, who crowd together, all watching the stallion intently. For a few moments he is motionless, then he neighs again and takes a few wild bounds forward before coming to a halt. He snorts, paws the ground and strikes out with his fore-hooves. All the horses look towards the horizon where another stallion can be seen, approaching at full gallop. He has scented the mares and is coming to try to take some of them for himself.

The herd stallion drums with his hooves and jumps into the air. His muscles tauten, and he draws on all his reserves of strength. The stranger approaches rapidly and the master rushes out to meet him, mouth wide open and teeth bared.

They rear up facing each other, breast to breast. One jumps high in the air, turning and biting; the other lashes out with tremendous force. Both snap viciously at each other's genitals. The two horses have become nothing but a writhing mass of muscle – turning, twisting, spinning . . . The air is filled with the sharp sounds of jaws snapping together on emptiness and the dull thuds of hooves striking cruppers and flanks. Wounds trail blood from their necks and the hollows of their knees, but the stallions

Left, *three young Lipizzaner stallions using the language of the nose. As they grow older they will become progressively lighter until their coats are the famous Lipizzaner white.*

Below, *two young Camargue mares stand watching impassively as their future mates fight.*

fight on, oblivious to the pain. . . .

Motionless, the mares and foals watch.

Rage ebbs from the two stallions as they realize they are equally matched, and they change tactics. At full gallop they rush at the herd, biting at the mares to force them to take flight. The mares are confused, not knowing which way to turn. One stallion drives them in one direction while the other urges them in another. The whole herd is in turmoil – stallions, mares and foals together. Whenever the two rivals meet they resume their fight with undiminished ferocity.

Finally the mares and foals all gallop off, and

the two stallions stop fighting to pursue them. The rivals run in among the mares to separate them out. Their posture changes, so that they become more like predators: the neck stretches forwards, the head is lowered almost to the ground, the ears are laid flat back against the skull. They compete fiercely to drive off as many mares as possible for themselves.

Eventually the struggle is over. The master of the herd has lost four of his eighteen mares to the rival.

Fights like this, while not infrequent in the wild, are rarely otherwise seen these days as most herds are under the partial or total protection of human beings. In the civilized sphere of horse-breeding the stallion has his isolated stud-box and the mares are led to him individually: this is essential among Thoroughbreds – especially race-horses – because it is vital to the breeder to know when to expect the birth of a new foal.

Left, *two Camargue stallions battle savagely, tails lashing and teeth snapping, for supremacy in the herd. Squealing, they rear to strike and bite their opponent until, the battle over, the loser* (below) *concedes the issue and gallops off, head and tail held high.*

In semi-wild herds, however, there are frequent minor clashes between the stallions but they are not life-or-death affairs. The geldings, too, may occasionally turn their backs on each other and let fly with their hooves. What is happening is that the young stallions are preparing themselves for an adult role which most of them will never need to play; or that the geldings are establishing a revised order of precedence within the herd, or are simply working off accumulated aggression. This last point is important: horses which are stabled on their own can become quite neurotic if they are not able, from time to time, to take out their pent-up aggression on something. Within the herd there is always another horse to kick out at or chase away.

Although mares seem to observe fights between stallions quite passively, this does not mean that they are not involved in what is going on. Sometimes their interest seems to be only transitory, but often enough they are watching with close attention, ready to react appropriately depending upon the outcome of the fight.

Even in a settled group, where a single stallion has a harem of mares, mating does not take place in any random fashion. Stallion and mares are

constantly in close proximity and, as the stallion drives the mares, he also smells them: the evidence of their scent will tell him when the time to cover is exactly right. This is useful knowledge – mares respond violently to approaches from stallions when their hormones tell them that the time is inappropriate. Young, inexperienced stallions take all kinds of punishment as the mares lash out viciously with their rear hooves, finding painful targets on their suitor's ribs and chest: the young stallions will grimly put up with this treatment; but the older ones will have learnt to keep out of the way until the time is exactly right.

In fact, mating is a risky business for all concerned. Should a mare approach a stallion who does not want her, he will drive her away with some force – so that she may trip or dash straight into bushes and thorns or, all too often these days, a barbed-wire fence. And the mares can be pretty vicious with each other, too. Sexual jealousy among them is often expressed with snapping teeth and flashing hooves. It is little wonder that wild horses in the aftermath of mating can look somewhat the worse for wear.

Like most other mammals, the mares have clearly defined periods of oestrus during which they are receptive to the stallions; at other times they are incapable of conceiving and will repel any advances. Their periods of heat last about 4 to 10 days and are repeated fairly regularly at intervals of 21–23 days. When in season they can display a markedly different character from usual:

Left, the changing moods of the weather seem not to concern the horses, but of course they are constantly aware of them. Below, a sunbeam spotlights a brown mare, singling her out from this herd of Hungarian horses quietly grazing.

they may be nervous and irritable or, conversely, unusually gentle; while in some cases there is no perceptible change of behaviour at all.

Once impregnated the mare carries her foal for 11 months, or, on average, 333 days. The healthier and more robust the mother, the better the chances of a problem-free birth, unless the father was of markedly larger stock. Complications are more likely to arise among domesticated horses than among wild ones.

Normally the birth takes place quite quickly – which is fortunate, because in the wild the delivery represents a peak danger-period for both mother and foal. Although in reality the potential hazards nowadays are few, the mare displays a primeval awareness of the fact that, while she is giving birth, she is unable to take flight from anything which might threaten her, be it fire, wild animals or hunters. Thus even in domesticated herds the mares prefer to give birth to their foals at night, alone and in a reassuringly familiar part of their territory – and preferably without human assistance. Generally speaking

Above, an American Saddle Horse stallion. As the name suggests, the Americans created this breed, and they have every right to be proud of it. This specimen fetched $100,000 in the 1970s from a South African buyer.

such assistance is not required: the mare knows instinctively what to do during and after the birth.

And there, in the morning, is the newborn foal.

Springtime
Mares normally foal-down during the spring and early summer, but in a sense the process of giving birth started the previous year. Most obviously, it began with the act of mating; but there were other, more subtle, preparations in progress as well.

During the summer and early autumn all the horses of the herd will endeavour to eat well enough to lay down a healthy layer of fat on which to draw during the winter: then, when the fresh green grass of the new spring arrives, the horses will be lean and trim, unencumbered by old fat. This cycle is particularly important for the mares, who during the cold months must feed the foals they are carrying from their own internal reserves. If the winter has been especially hard, the mares may have lost some of their own body-weight, but by the time of foaling-down they will at least partially have replaced their reserves by

Left, flared nostrils sniffing the air, a young chestnut stallion, as yet untried, gazes out at the exciting world. All his senses are on the alert for any possible threat or unexpected danger. Young and proud, he is surely destined to be the sire of many of his breed.

eating the fresh spring vegetation. The lush grasses are rich in all the nutrients required to assist the mare in the production of the milk on which she will feed her new offspring. Well fed but still lean and fit, she should give birth easily and, soon afterwards, resume her normal pattern of behaviour. Mares in domestication which are well fed all the year round are in fact being overfed during the winter months: they tend to have difficulty in conceiving, and often spontaneously abort their foetuses during the first few weeks of pregnancy.

As soon as the foal is born the mare starts to lick it systematically all over with her rough tongue. She takes the dampness from its coat, which sticks to the tiny body in waves and curls, and she rubs her tongue over the sturdy legs with their protuberant joints. In so doing she is not only licking the foal dry: she is licking it warm. Only minutes before it was snug in her womb, and so it needs the vigorous friction of her tongue to get its blood-circulation moving strongly.

Over the next few days the foal will turn from a helpless newborn creature into a young horse. Most of the changes that take place we can observe – we can see it, for example, learning how to use its legs and to run – but there is one important development which is essential if the foal is to become truly a horse. It must discover something which foals born in stables are usually denied: to follow the herd. It must learn to move fearlessly and confidently by the side of its mother, whatever the surroundings, and to obey the calls of the leading mare or stallion and the warnings given to the herd by the sentries. A foal on its own or isolated with its mother will never be a true horse: it can be fulfilled only if it is part of the herd.

We started this chapter by commenting that, when you look at a herd of wild horses, you are looking back into time. But in a rather different sense, as you watch a herd grazing peacefully, with its young foals gambolling about or contentedly feeding alongside their mothers, you are looking forward in time as well. Those foals are the future of the herd: the lessons they learn during their first spring and summer will ensure the survival of the herd in the coming years, when their parents are long gone. Like the cells of a single body, the members of the herd have renewed themselves.

Left, *this little Arab mare will fix her good looks on her progeny. No trace of inferior blood here . . .*

This Døle Trotter (right), *by contrast, may lack 'breeding', but he and his sort have proved true friends to mankind.*

FROM BIRTH TO A YEARLING

The natural state of a horse is to be part of a herd, whether it be a truly wild herd, a herd of horses that have gone wild, or a herd living a comparatively sheltered existence under the general care of human beings. For thousands of years, nomads, farmers and breeders saw no reason to interfere with this natural order of things: when you wanted a horse you went and got one, but otherwise the animals lived much as they would have had mankind never existed. Nobody thought of studbooks, or registers, or documents to establish parentage. The different races of horses, which we distinguish readily by their physical appearance, temperament and so on, first developed as a result of evolutionary adaptation to the prevailing environmental conditions. Human beings might bring together stallions and mares of different types in order to try to produce offspring particularly well suited to specific tasks, such as hunting, warfare or agriculture; but in general terms the horse was still very much a product of nature.

During the eighteenth and, most significantly, the nineteenth century this all changed. At first only in a few countries were systems developed whereby stallions were registered and mares collected together in stud-farms, with careful documentation of their progeny. Today, however, controlled breeding is carried out in virtually every part of the world – although details of the procedure vary considerably from country to country. Sometimes the State takes overall control of the breeding arrangements and selects the stallions which are to be used as sires; more typically, this selection is the task of breeding associations who at any given time will be looking after and promoting the interests of a single race of horses. In some countries only registered horses are allowed to participate in various sporting events, such as dressage or flat-racing. Matters of registration are of very little importance to the person who simply enjoys riding horses, but it is very likely that the horse you normally ride belongs not to a natural race but to a manmade

one. Within only a couple of hundred years mankind has wrought a profound change in the evolutionary course of the horse.

You have only to look at a modern pure-bred horse to see how different it is from the wild animals that were its forebears. The stallion pictured on page 25 is an American Saddle Horse – in fact, it is one of the premier individuals in a breed which is held in especial reverence. This horse was bred in isolation, and a rider was carefully selected to train him to walk in five distinct gaits – walk, trot, canter, slow-gait (stepping pace) and rack. He has been fastidiously groomed: the hair on his head has been plaited into a glossy red-and-white band, and his mane has been clipped off six inches (15 cm) behind the sickle-shaped ears in order to display the over-long neck to better advantage. He has never been treated in any way which might alarm him or even make him mildly anxious: you could say that he has been spoilt. He is a stallion tailor-made to be admired in the showring, not to fight, savage and raging, with his rivals for mares.

The Døle Trotter pictured on page 27 is another horse that has been created by mankind, but he could hardly be more different. He is a working companion – a friend, even – rather than an object to be admired. His head is sturdy and a little heavy, his thick long hair falls over his forehead, and the hair of his mane is somewhat matted and frizzled. He's a farmer's horse, pure and simple, serving his master by drawing the cart and the plough, taking the family to church on a Sunday or to market on the other days. He's good-natured, always ready to work, and rarely ill.

In a way, these two horses lie at the extremes of the manmade breeds – the elegant dandy and the patient toiler – and there are innumerable other different 'artificial races' of horse in between. All of these types of horse can interbreed at will and

The time is exactly right for mating, and so the stallion mounts the mare.

generally without any complications unless the stallion is of far bigger stock than the mare, in which case she may have a troublesome time of it when foaling. Over the years, mankind has learned to take advantage of this in order to produce horses which are very different from their ancestors.

Covering
Today, in the West at least, mares are almost without exception covered in one of two ways: either in the herd (see page 23), or by being led by hand to the stallion. This latter method is nowadays by far the more usual. When in the stable, the valuable stallion is always under control, and his feeding can be regulated according to the circumstances. He is available whenever he is required, and the breeder will bring the mare to him only when he knows that the time is right. In order to avoid any possibility of the stallion being injured through the mare kicking out at him, her rear legs may be secured with a hobble, or some kind of protective barrier may be used. The whole process of covering is under strict human control, and the stallion doesn't need to exert himself more than is absolutely necessary; he can cover a large number of mares during the course of a single season, and they can be taken straight home again after having been covered with a minimum of trouble.

In short, everything here is extremely convenient – for the humans. It is a rather different story for the horses, though, as shown by the fact that the fertility rate is very much lower than when they are allowed to mate in more natural circumstances. Quite often a mare which will not conceive under artificial constraints will become pregnant quite quickly when allowed to run with the stallion. Still, most breeders feel that the advantages of controlled matings more than outweigh the disadvantages.

In order to be sure that the timing is as favourable as possible, the breeder will carry out a test on the mare. Either the planned sire or a substitute stallion employed specially for the purpose – known as a 'teaser' – is allowed to sniff at the mare, either from his stall or in a testing-frame. If she responds by kicking out and uttering loud, unwilling cries, then it is too soon. When she is ready to accept the stallion, however, she will stand quite still as he approaches.

It is interesting to watch a stallion's behaviour at this time. As soon as the mare's scent reaches his nostrils he blows them open, pushes his head

Is there something in the wind? The stallion demonstrates the facial expressions and grimaces that are often the prelude to mating activities.

Irish Connemara mares left out with the stallion so that their mating can take place as nature intended.

forwards so that his hair flies up, and grimaces. This grimacing is primarily a sign of sexuality, although it happens at other times, too. He raises his head upwards, and off to one side; his ears adopt something of a central position between the forward bent of attentiveness and the backward rake of distrust. He closes his nostrils and holds his teeth shut, while his upper lip is drawn upwards and the lower lip downwards. He holds this position while taking another deep breath. If he was right the first time, if that really *is* the scent of a mare on heat, he naturally associates it with the mating act. His neck muscles tighten and from his half-open mouth emerges a mysterious, soft, full whinny. This sound is his way of showing his discovery of something pleasing, and is quite different from the clear trumpeting of the attack, the shrill bad-tempered screech of anger or the loud calls which horses use to communicate with each other in the herd. All is now set for the covering to proceed.

The First Hours of Life

As previously remarked, covering in the herd is much more natural and easy, and the same is true of the resulting birth some 11 months later. The further a mare's life is from nature, the more likely it is that there will be complications in the birth. It is ironic that, although it is much easier for human help to be supplied to a mare giving birth in a stable, if she were giving birth instead in the meadow where she spent most of her life she almost certainly wouldn't need the help!

Mares about to foal in a stable should be given a specially large, clean stall, banked at the sides with straw. As soon as the mother has given birth to the foal, she will lick it as it lies there on the straw, drying off the amniotic fluid still covering its body. It is like watching magic at work: at one moment you have a damp, helpless shape on the straw, the next there is a small living being, already alert and beginning to think about trying to stand up to see what life is all about.

This is the beginning of the foal's second big adventure: first it was born and now, so soon after, it must try to stand up on legs that have never before supported anything; legs that seem to be too long, with too many joints which have a

A stranger in a strange world. However, it will be a matter of only a few minutes before the newborn foal will have struggled to his feet.

nasty habit of giving way at unexpected moments. However, foals, like other young animals, are programmed in advance to follow a quite definite pattern of behaviour: they must stand up and learn how to master those cumbersome, spidery legs just as quickly as possible. This is because horses are 'designed' to be born in the wild, not in stables. If danger threatens their only response is flight, and the sooner the newborn foals can learn to join in that flight the better. There is therefore an imperative instruction built into the foal's brain: stand up and find out as quickly as you can how to run away, just in case you need to.

So the foal keeps on trying to sort out its legs and make sense of its feet. It falls over quite a lot, but each time immediately has another try. In an improbably short time it succeeds, and stands there unsteadily, trembling and panting. But it stays like this for only a moment; then come its first few experimental steps. In a way, it hasn't really been born properly until it has learned how

to walk – even if at this stage it is more of a stagger than a walk.

Only now does the foal start to exhibit an instinctive behavioural pattern familiar to other animals including humans. While stumbling about it stretches out its mouth and makes a small bag with its lips. It smacks its lips . . . and finds nothing; but it goes on trying. Although its mother is by now standing alongside, she will not help it find the teat: she is more concerned with trying to lick those parts of the foal's body which are still wet, and she will nudge it around a little, if necessary, in order to get at those parts.

No, the job of finding the udder in order to take its first feed is the foal's alone. However, just as the urge to get to its feet and walk was imprinted on it, so is the basic information as to how to find the source of food. Suddenly the foal 'remembers' where to look, and in moments has its lips wrapped around one of its mother's teats and is sucking firmly.

The first milk of the foal's life is incredibly important, for not only does it contain all the nutrients which the foal needs, it is also rich in the mother's antibodies, white blood cells and other immunity-promoting materials. Without this 'cocktail' of defensive agents the foal would have no defence against infection in the early days before its own immune system gets going, and would be extremely vulnerable to any infection that might be around. This first milk is called colostrum, and it serves the same vital function in other mammals, including humans.

The mother may now begin to take a more active part in the foal's training – if, that is, both mother and foal are allowed out of the stable to run free in the meadow. This course is advisable because, apart from allowing the foal an important part of its early education, there is much less risk of contracting an infection from its surroundings in the stable. Within an hour or two of being put out, the mare will have coaxed or bullied the foal into running around and following her everywhere. The mother, of course, has a unique means of persuading the foal to do all these things: she is the one with the food.

Lessons learnt by the foal during these early training sessions will stand it in good stead all the days of its life. It will discover that three legs will keep it up if one should fail, that stumbling can be averted if the balance of the body is right, and that every piece of rough ground needn't necessarily represent a hazard: foals who learn these things early will go on to become much more sure-footed cross-country horses later in life, when they carry riders. At a less obvious level, the foal also learns very quickly to acclimatize to the weather: if it is running around in rain or a keen wind at this stage it will be much less concerned about inclement weather conditions when it is older. Nowadays, fortunately, most

The new foal sucks while the mother finishes her job of cleaning it up, a job she does instinctively.

breeders have seen the wisdom of this: the stable may be a snugger haven, but the young animal cannot live in a stable all of its life.

Of course, the breeder can have some say in the weather conditions which the young horse is likely to face. It doesn't take much ingenuity to ensure that foals are born in spring or early summer, when the weather can be expected to be reasonably friendly. However, in the case of Thoroughbreds, this is rarely done – for reasons connected with racing. Thoroughbreds are described as 'yearlings' for racing purposes until the second January 1st after their birth – that is to say, a foal born on January 2nd will be a yearling until it is one day short of two years old, whereas one born on December 31st will stop being a yearling after only a year and a day. The breeder of Thoroughbreds will therefore do his or her best to ensure that foals are born shortly after January 1st. Breeders of other horses need not be affected by such artificial constraints, and should be able to plan things so that each young foal gets its early training sessions with its mother in the fresh air and comfortable temperatures of April or May.

The other horses look on with interest, but the foal stays close by its mother's side.

Mother and Child

The relationship between mare and foal is a powerful bond which lasts for some time and is capable of being adapted to meet special external requirements. Unlike a predator such as the wolf, which leaves its young in the lair while it hunts for food for itself and, once they are weaned, for the litter as well, the mare never needs to be separated from her foal. It can run along beside her, assuming she doesn't go too fast, jumping over obstacles and feeding directly from her until it is able to graze independently, although still alongside her.

It is interesting to watch the way in which a herd community receives a newborn foal. Immediately after the birth, all the mares crowd around the newcomer and absorb its scent. This is important, because in any future time of danger they must know that it is a part of their group. Nowadays, of course, such dangers probably won't come along, but horses respond to instincts which have been implanted in them over millions of years of evolution, not to the experiences of the last few thousand years. Even mares which are kept in isolation will display a lively interest in the newborn foals of others and, if allowed to, will nuzzle them and take their scent.

Young foals are enchanting creatures. In order

to grow up in a proper 'horse' fashion they should be allowed to spend their first year of life out in the meadow in the company of as many horses and other foals as possible. It's fun to watch as they tumble around, falling over and clambering up again, imitating their mothers as they take their first, experimental nibble of grass. In fact, in all this apparently purposeless play a number of important instincts are at work – the most notable of which is the 'flight reaction'.

No matter how often a foal falls over it will still keep on trying to do things right, showing no signs of being dispirited by these reversals. It is blessed with that astonishing energy which drives on the young of all running creatures from the time of their birth. So far as the foal's instincts are concerned, its well-being will always rely upon immediate, lightning-fast flight, so the reactions of even the youngest and smallest horse must be quick and powerful. The foal, although we must be careful of the fallacy of giving it human intelligence and characteristics, is relentlessly driving itself on to become a stronger, healthier and more efficient flight-taking machine. Even though its exercises are dressed up in a form which *we* see as play, they are powered by an energy that is in essence fuelled by dread – dread of possible hazards, such as those which threatened its forebears over the long period of equine evolution.

What were at first clumsy, graceless movements are gradually smoothed out as the foal becomes more nimble and assured. It will romp about, perform series of staccato vertical jumps and – what is slightly bizarre to watch – often follow these up with a somersault. Quite why this trick should be stored up in its racial memory is something of a mystery. It will race along with its head outstretched, and perform abrupt, frighteningly sharp twists and bends – with each fresh outburst of energy being rewarded by a drink of its mother's milk. It is learning how to escape from danger.

A less important but nevertheless potent instinct is rolling. When a horse rolls on the ground the action not only helps to clean its coat of major superficial dirt but also loosens its muscles and joints. The sight of foals rolling on the ground can spark off a chain-reaction in the herd. At first the adult horses look on casually, but then, one after the other, heads sink to the ground, noses investigate scents . . . The horses wander around, sniffing the ground – especially where other horses have been rolling – until they find a suitable spot; then they crash to the ground and

indulge in an orgy of rolling. First they rub one side enthusiastically against the ground; then they stretch all four legs happily into the air and give their spines the treatment; finally they do the other side.

Horses enjoy rolling in sand, in mud, in snow and on grass; in adult years they derive especial pleasure from rolling around while still wet with sweat after having been ridden. They prefer it to any other form of cleaning, and clearly enjoy carrying around the hard layer of encrusted mud which they gather. Finally they stand up, stretch their necks forward, stiffen their backs, set their feet firmly and shake themselves so that the sand, dust or snow flies off in clouds. Of course, to a human being they still seem pretty dirty after all

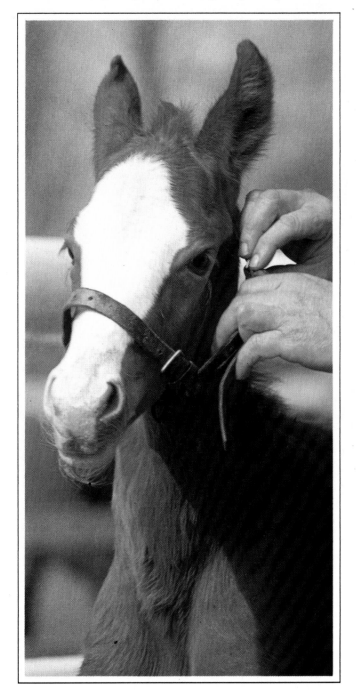

The foal should be allowed to become accustomed to human handling as early as possible. This one shows no fear.

Left, this proud mother is very likely already in foal again, as brood mares under natural circumstances will regularly bear one foal a year.

Above, the foal's legs are long in proportion to the rest of the body – and sometimes they seem almost too long!

this, but the whole rolling exercise has satisfied the cleansing requirements of the horse – and, after all, you can always brush the dried dust off him before taking him out for a ride.

It is likewise important that foals learn how to graze, although this is not as simple as it sounds. Foals have proportionately short necks by comparison with adult horses. The short neck makes it easy to suckle from the mare, but it makes reaching for grass very much more difficult, especially when the foal's legs are still less than one hundred per cent reliable. Moreover, those legs are still too long for easy grazing – they are designed, at this stage, purely to facilitate the foal's flight from potential danger. With its short neck and its overlong legs, the foal will perform some astonishing contortions in order to get its head close enough to the ground to champ at the grass. Many of these contortions are unsuccessful – and, anyway, at this early stage it doesn't matter much, since the foal's primary source of food is still its mother's milk: its digestive system

has yet to adapt itself for grass. In due course, as the animal grows older, the proportions of its body will change such that grazing becomes a comfortable, natural business.

As summer advances the foals grow up among the buttercups and daisies and gradually become more self-reliant; if they are living among other horses they will be learning the rules of the herd, too. Still standing close to their mothers, they begin to concentrate their attentions more on the other foals. Life has been good to them thus far and they feel pretty secure, so they pluck up the courage to take a few tentative steps towards each other. The mothers watch all this placidly, not interfering: they know that, if they call, the foal will return immediately. For the foals already have a good grasp of the system of command and instruction within the herd. They obey their mothers' calls. If the leading mare calls, then the whole family will go to her. If a higher-ranking mare calls, she will be obeyed. Everybody obeys the stallion, if there is one. Any act of disobedience is punished by the next higher-ranking mare with bites, threatening noises and kicks.

Even when foals have spent the whole of their

Overleaf, all foals are enchanting, whether they are woolly wild ones or sleek Thoroughbreds. The sun on their backs is good for them . . . and they love to roll.

lives in the same meadow as each other, and know one another by sight, their first mutual approaches are cautious. The horse is in all respects a cautious animal. They approach one another step by step, but don't go too close and certainly not close enough at first to rub noses; it will be a few days before they are confident enough for that. The other foal *looks* reassuringly like a friend, but is that enough? In the end, after many abortive attempts, the two noses make soft, trembling contact . . . although even the distant snapping of a twig will be enough to send both foals scurrying back in a beeline to the safety of their mother's side.

Naturally, in the end friendship is established. Horses do like to associate with others of their own kind, after all. But until the bond is made, the foals sniff at each other rather a lot, make sure that their intentions are friendly, and keep a watchful eye open to make certain that mother is

Above, *young animals are eternally curious. These two are making friends and will soon be gambolling together.*

Right, *foals rarely move from their mother's side: she is, after all, the source of both food and comfort.*

never too far away.

All this time the foals are growing more independent. In the same way that they have learned to feed on grass and twigs rather than rely on their mothers' milk, they also learn to depend upon their own self-confidence rather than having always to fly to mother. And mother, too, is beginning to grow away from them. For practical reasons, breeders will separate the foals from the mares when they are not less than five or six months old, and healthy young horses will get over this breach without too many problems: perhaps a single day of shock and distress before

it is all forgotten. In the wild, the probability is that the mare is already carrying her next foal. If, in the coming winter, she has enough food to be able to convert some into milk she will give occasional feeds to the still-growing foal; but in the succeeding spring she will drive it away quite harshly, if necessary with bites and kicks. Her concern now is the accumulation of adequate reserves of food to cope with the new foal, which will be arriving very soon.

It is impossible at this stage to say how the foal will turn out. As the old saying goes, only fools judge foals . . .

A full year has gone by in the life of the herd. The young foals born last spring are now independent young horses in their own right. They are still not fully grown, of course. It will be another two years before they can safely be put under the saddle, and in some breeds it may even be another four years. But the foals have learned their relative status among the other horses and, while they are not capable of a completely independent existence in isolation – they will never achieve that – they are at least independent of their mothers, interacting with other horses of all ages and preparing to become the parents of succeeding generations of the herd.

WORKING HORSES

In earliest times, man hunted horses as a source of meat. We know this for certain, because in Stone Age cave-dwellings accumulations of horse-bones have been found which had been split open to extract the marrow. Also, cave-paintings exist showing people hunting down horses with spears. In fact, the horse was an admirably convenient source of food for our ancestors, because those early human beings were, like the horses, nomadic. It was a simple matter for the tribes of humans to follow the herds, picking off animals for meat and possibly milking the mares – although this latter must have been a more dangerous business. Perhaps our Neolithic forebears also experimented with keeping horses in herds in much the same way, and for much the same reasons, as people have for millennia kept herds of cattle.

But it can't have been long before primitive man discovered that you can do more with this big, strong, docile animal than simply eat it: you can make it work, either by getting it to pull loads or by persuading it to take a load on its back. Once again, we can tell from cave-paintings that our ancestors invented the halter very early on, and had realized that they could get from place to place with much less effort and much more quickly by sitting astride a horse. Another early invention was a primitive sledge which consisted of two long poles tied at one end on either side of the horse and rigged up at the other to take a load that would have been too heavy for the horse to carry on its back. The addition of wheels to produce the first carts was a natural development, and allowed the horse to pull still heavier loads.

Exactly where in the world the first domestication of the horse took place is uncertain, but it is generally held that it was among either the Chinese or the Indian Brahmans; in fact, according to the Brahman version of Hinduism, the very first human being was set astride a horse. We know that by 3500 BC, if not millennia before, the Chinese had mastered the basic principles of horsemanship; and soon afterwards these tech-

niques were widespread throughout all parts of the world where the horse could be found. All of the well known early civilizations made use of the horse either for transport and agriculture or, all too often, for war. The Assyrians were able to come down 'like a wolf on the fold' because of their cavalry skills; they had become expert horsemen by about 2500 BC, if not earlier. The Egyptians were, surprisingly, slow on the uptake; although they used horses to draw light chariots for sport and warfare from about 1500 BC or earlier, they relegated the task of *riding* horses to slaves and the lower classes, to the servants responsible for looking after the chariot-horses.

From as long ago as 1600 BC a cuneiform document on clay survives dealing with the care and maintenance of horses. This particular document was Hittite, but presumably other cultures produced similar 'manuals' which have failed to survive. A rather tangled trail of deduction from Greek mythology suggests that, very early on, ocean-going conquerors had learned how to transport their cavalries on board ship. According to the myths, the first horse had been created by Poseidon, the sea-god, and had emerged splashing from the waves (the name 'Pegasus' can be translated as 'born out of the ocean'), and this is rather reminiscent of horses being disembarked in the shallows and ridden up onto the beach by invading hordes.

The first 'modern' treatises on horsemanship appeared in about 400 BC from the pen of Xenophon: they were the *Hipparchus* (a guide for cavalry commanders) and the *Cynegeticus* (a guide to hunting). Much of their content remains perfectly valid today. Some time earlier, the Sybarites had developed a primitive form of dressage: their famous 'dancing horses' performed to music. Legend has it that these animal entertainers caused the downfall of the Sybarites in one of their periodic wars with the neighbouring Crotons: in the height of battle, the Crotons started playing suitable music and the Sybaritic cavalry was abruptly reduced to absolute confusion.

Mongolian herdsmen have been catching their horses in the same way since time immemorial. They use an urga, *a flexible pole with a leather noose at the end – a device which is similar in use to the lasso. Very often you find that herdsmen in widely separated parts of the world have independently devised similar solutions to similar problems.*

The Mongolian festival called Nadom is a time for the exchange of news and views. The highlights are the mounted competitions.

Another historical item which is almost certainly apocryphal is that the abhorrent Roman Emperor Caligula in about AD 30–40 created his horse Incitatus a priest and consul, giving it wine from a golden goblet and bedding it in a cot of ivory.

Be that as it may, the horse was clearly of very great significance in the lives of the earliest peoples, for horses play a great part in most if not all Western mythologies. The Greeks' Pegasus we have already noted. In Scandinavian mythology one finds Odin's eight-legged horse Sleipnir, which could traverse the sea as easily as the land, and the steed Skinfaxi – 'Shining Mane' – which

drew the car of day to make sure that the Sun came up each morning and sank to the horizon each night. At nights Hrimfaxi – 'Frosty Mane' – held sway: from its bit fell the drops of rime that bedewed the world during the hours of darkness. Persian mythology featured Shibdiz, a war-charger fleeter than the wind. In a much more recent mythology, the collection of Arthurian legends, we find horses playing an important role: according to one tradition, Arthur's own horse was called Spumador, the 'Foaming One', presumably in reference to its speed and stamina. Horses feature also in the visual arts of all the relevant nations – in mosaics and paintings, on vases, goblets and even coins.

All of these horses were, strictly speaking, working horses.

An Ancient Partnership

The most famous horse-user of historical times was Genghis Khan, whose Mongol hordes during the thirteenth century swept all before them in a huge swathe from the Black Sea to the Pacific; paradoxically, they simultaneously spread a form of benevolent civilization while committing acts of almost unimaginable barbarity. We get a fairly clear picture of those horsemen of 700 years ago from contemporary accounts, but we get an even clearer one from looking at the Mongolian peoples of today and their relationship with the horse, for not a lot has changed – except that they no longer make a practice of conquering Asia!

The horses ridden by the Khans' hordes were rather different from those we know today. Evidence suggests that they were small, muscular, powerful animals with short straight necks and sinewy legs. According to the accounts, these horses could run like the wind, swim like otters, climb like goats, gallop for days on end, endure incredible extremes of heat and cold, and so on. Much of this was undoubtedly exaggeration, born from the astonishment of peoples who had never seen anything like it all before (one thinks of the reactions of some of the Amerindians to their first sight of mounted riders, whom they believed to be centaurs; and indeed the Greek legend of the centaurs was probably a result of a similar mis-

Overleaf, more than a thousand horses are gathered together, but these days the purpose is to enjoy mounted competitions rather than to organize for battle.

understanding millennia earlier). However, to a great extent it was true. The Mongols' horses seem to have been like the Przewalski's Horse, *Equus Przewalskii*, itself regarded as a 'carbon copy' of the fossil ancestor of all modern horses. The Mongol horses were tough beasts, if so, having survived virtually unchanged since the end of the world's last major glaciation, 10,000 or so years ago.

And we can be certain, too, that in Genghis Khan's armies the soldiers were virtually inseparable from their horses, because that is still the case in Mongolia today. As a matter of everyday routine they perform actions which, in the more 'civilized' countries of the West, would be regarded with awe as impressive circus tricks. For thousands of years these people have lived in the closest possible partnership with their horses.

The herdsmen catch their horses in exactly the same way as they did thousands of years ago, using a device called an urga: this is a long flexible pole with a leather noose at the end, and is the equivalent of the cowboys' lasso. What happens is that the herdsmen ride trained horses – 'catchers' – which follow the wild ones at a set distance, chasing them into a previously determined position where the rider can easily slip the noose of the urga over the fugitive's neck. The catcher then halts, so that all the wild horse does as it struggles is to cut off its own air-supply. The catchers,

interestingly enough, seem to find the whole sport every bit as exhilarating as do the herdsmen astride them.

In late spring or early summer the Mongolians have their traditional festival of Nadom, and people ride for days or even weeks to take part in the festivities. Food is plentiful and the horses are nicely rounded thanks to the new season's grass. Guest tents are set up and the race-tracks are marked out; preparations are made for wrestling matches and archery contests. The high-spots of the festivals are the contests to find out who has the best horse, who is the best bowman, and so on.

The Nadom races are run over distances of 12½–50 miles (20–80 km). The equine qualities which interest the Mongolians are endurance, stamina and toughness, so any shorter distance would not be worth racing, as far as they're concerned. The riders are children aged up to 10 years; their feet are tied together with a rope which runs under the stomachs of the saddleless horses. The spectators, also mounted, spread out over the surrounding hills and enthusiastically

Canadian cattle are only rarely driven as hard as this or they would lose too much flesh and condition.

support the competitors. The winning horse is given a triumphant reception – its jockey going largely ignored!

Of course, the Mongolians do not make a general practice of riding bareback. For Western riders the short-stirruped Mongolian saddles would be extremely uncomfortable. The rider has to support himself on his knees, like a jockey, leaning forward into the wind as the horse moves at a gallop. The Berbers of North Africa ride in a similar fashion, as do the Andalusians, the style bearing the stamp of 700 years of Arab/Berber rule. This riding posture is found only in countries where the horses are very fleet of foot, the riders showing an inborn sense of perfect balance.

Mongolian saddles are very valuable, and are passed down from father to son through the generations. They have leather inlays and are decorated with colourful ornamentation; a pad of felt or skin cushions the wooden seat. The bridle consists of a finely plaited halter with small side-loops which can hold a snaffle-bit.

If the Mongolians provide us with a living replica of the relationship between ancient peoples and their horses, others of the world's cultures which have been comparatively little affected by the 'benefits' of Western civilization survive to show us an exactly opposite attitude to the horse. For example in Australia, where herds of wild horses ('brumbies') have roamed for the past two hundred years, the native Aborigines still prefer to go on foot. In Africa, the horse never really travelled across the Equator until the nineteenth century, when the Boers brought it to Africa's southernmost tip. And in America, although the Plains Indians took to the horse enthusiastically, as so many Western movies show us, most Amerindian tribes neither went on horseback nor used the horse for agriculture.

By contrast, other peoples adopted the horse with such astonishing rapidity that it seemed almost as if they had been just waiting for it to come along. The Indians of Mexico and of the western parts of North America had become completely horse-oriented within a few short decades of the animal's introduction to the New World. Interestingly, they independently developed the old Asiatic sledge mentioned on page

43; women and children and the sick were transported on it during the nomadic wanderings of the tribes. The Basuto of what is now called Lesotho in Africa saw the horse for the first time in the 1820s, when the Boers used it in their bloody struggles with the Black indigenous peoples, but within about 40 years this Bantu people had taken to the horse so comprehensively that they became known as the 'Indians of Africa'.

Pack-horses

Among the Amerindians, the Basuto and the Mongols, the horse has never really seen much use as a draught animal, for the primary reason that there were (and often still are) no roads suitable for wagons. To get the best out of wagons, a culture requires a network of level, fairly wide tracks and predominantly flat country. Where there are marshes, forests, streams and rivers, mountains, scree slopes and so on, and where the population is sparse, there is little incentive to indulge in road-building. Accordingly, rather than use the horse to pull wagons, the people tend to concentrate instead on using it as a pack animal. Even today in Lesotho there are comparatively few roads, and these are mostly around the frontiers; in the interior you meet caravans of pack-horses that have changed little since the days when other cultures used them to supply the furthest corners of the known world.

In hot countries the horse shares its burden with dromedaries, donkeys and so on; in colder regions either native ponies shoulder the burden alone or imported horses share it with animals such as yaks and llamas. In northern India, for example, you can still find Spiti ponies picking their way safely along dizzily high paths and tolerating heat and dust, frost and ice with placid equanimity. In many parts of the world this millennia-old practice of using long chains of pack-horses is still going strong, and not just in the less developed countries. In Spain, for example, many of the wayside *posadas* (inns) still have stabling for the hundreds of pack animals that until quite recently used to haul ores and trading goods through the sierras. In many ways, this is still the most convenient way of transporting such goods around.

But pack-horses were not confined to the high mountain passes. Mankind took this wild, free-running creature into the bowels of the Earth to carry goods along mineshafts or to haul wagons filled with coal or ore. These horses could spend their entire lives – 18 to 20 years – without ever

It takes four to rope a calf – two men and two horses working in unison. The horses take it all in their stride, peacefully grazing once the calf has been thrown.

knowing fresh air or the scent of a grassy meadow. But they survived in their hundreds of thousands. At least they had the two most important prerequisites, food and shelter, and a regular regime of hard work to occupy them. For the horse is basically a simple animal which thrives on uniformly repeated activity which it can understand.

Thus, although we must be thankful that horses are no longer expected to live their lives underground, working under pressure for dismayingly long shifts, we have also to recognize that it was probably the very severity of their workload that kept them alive until old age. They were worked heavily, to be sure, but not quite too much. Conversely, it has to be recognized that underfeeding, insufficient care, too little training and of course overwork will quickly wear horses out. This was realized a long time ago. In the nineteenth century the British postal authorities, renowned in those days as a marvel of precision and speed, observed a rule that post-horses be retired after only three years of service. This had nothing to do with altruism: it was simply recognition that, after three years of intensely hard, unremitting work, the horses were no longer physically capable of taking the strain. Also in Britain, in the railway heavy-goods services, horses were retired after six years – despite excellent care and feeding and a judicious sharing-out of the workload, because continuous employment on metalled roads wore out their bones and joints.

Riding the Herds
On the other hand, the horses of herdsmen throughout the world are shining examples of what the animals are capable of when trained to become full collaborative partners, rather than drudges carrying out unsuitable, dull labour. Herding shows many basic similarities the world over: you will recall how similar the urga of the Mongolians was, in terms of use, to the lasso of the American cowboy. Both represent like solutions to an identical problem. We shall therefore concentrate here on herding as it is done in Canada, remembering that, while in other parts of the world the details of the practice will vary, the main principles will not.

The first thing to notice is that the riding style is quite different from anything that you will find in a riding school, simply because its purpose is

Left, *cutting out a single animal from the herd is specialist work, as the steer's instinct is to return to its fellows.*

Above right, *a Swiss farmer turns hay with his Freiberg mare.*
Below right, *ploughing with a Fjordling in Norway.*

With her foal still at foot, learning what it's all about, a Romanian mare draws the plough.

different. The cowboy, carrying his lasso in his right hand, has only his left with which to control the animal – and, quite frequently, he must also use his left hand for other work too. His riding of the horse is thus not an end in itself: he is using the horse as a vehicle, and the riding of it is merely a prerequisite for and accompaniment to the activities that are the central purpose for him being there at all. The horse therefore has to know how to react with the minimum of guidance and at all times to be aware of what is expected of it. It is trained to obey the subtlest of instructions, a process which requires much time and patience.

The North American cattle-herds were originally given complete freedom of pasture, and even today they are often confined in such vast areas that to all intents and purposes they are living in the wide open spaces of the prairies. It is part of the cowboys' skill to keep the animals of the herd together and to control them in such a way that they obtain sufficient fodder, find water supplies, and are given peace to ruminate. The cattle kept in these vast holdings are almost wild and are hardly ever handled.

We get a totally false impression, from cowboy movies, of how the men and horses go about the task of dealing with these wild creatures. The hero galloping furiously 'in all directions at once' (as Stephen Leacock would have it) around the herd is an image from the cinema screen, not a portrait of real life. The normal driving of herds involves no galloping at all: that would soon have the cattle moving too quickly, possibly stampeding out of control, and losing weight in the process, whereas the whole object of the exercise is to get the cattle to put on as much weight as possible. If the herd is grazing peacefully, then the job of the cowboy horse is to stand there motionlessly for hours on end. Its muscle-packed hindquarters will allow it to break into a short, swift sprint so that a steer that has separated from

Right, fresh horses being driven out to replace the morning shift tending the sheep on the South African karroo.

Overleaf, a Norwegian Fjord Horse takes tourists to see the spectacular Jostedalsbreen glacier, the largest in Europe.

the rest can be brought quickly back into the herd. Most of the other work is done at a peaceful walk.

Wherever herdsmen work with horses they use sharp bits and long, thin reins. These reins are scarcely gripped, being generally held between the two fingers of a hand. Turns are made by touching the horse's neck with the reins, and by the rider adjusting his weight in such a way as to communicate to the horse which way to go. Although controlling the animal like this requires a deep understanding of horses by the rider, the basic rules are easily learnt by both horse and human.

In North America the horses themselves are strong, compact Quarter-horses, about 14–15 hands high: they are regarded as the best cattle-horses in the world. Besides their physical advantages of strength and manoeuvrability, they are

also a useful medium size – not too big, not too small – and, most important of all, they have a 'cow sense' bred into them over the generations. They seem to have an instinctive 'feel' for working with cattle.

They use this cow sense above all in the work of 'cutting'. Cutting is the process of separating out an individual steer from the herd, manoeuvring it a certain distance away, and keeping it there for purposes of branding, inoculation, quarantine (if the steer is sick), and so on. Usually the job is done by cowboys working in pairs. They wait until the herd comes to a halt at some suitable place, and then goad the wanted steer into motion. Their two horses, which have been trained precisely for the task, run in such a way that they keep the wanted steer between them. At a suitable moment the rider of one horse will throw his lasso around the steer's neck and, at lightning speed, wind the other end around the high pommel of his saddle; his horse immediately engages its strength against that of the furious steer. The other rider runs his horse in such a way that he can cast the noose of his lasso around the steer's hindlegs. Both horses then immediately

Left, life is hard for a cab-horse in Kashmir, but the brighter his decoration the more chance of attacting customers.

Below, this little Syrian girl's pony is her constant friend, and she rides him seemingly instinctively.

The Garde Républicaine, *swords drawn, ride their chestnut horses along the boulevards of Paris.*

come to a complete halt, and the cow ends up on the ground. As it lies there, the two horses calmly retreat until both lines are taut. They are so cool and collected about this that they may even start to graze; but any suggestion that they have lost interest now that the job is done would be completely misplaced. They are constantly adjusting and readjusting their positions to keep the lines taut as the steer struggles. They do so without further instructions, leaving the cowboys free to tackle the steer. When cutting is demonstrated at rodeos (see page 135) the riders must hold their arms up in the air to show that it is the horse which is doing all the work.

Steers are probably the toughest animals that herdsmen have to handle. In South Africa's karroo, for example, horsemen have the far easier task of working with sheep. For much of the time the flocks graze undisturbed on vast farms; the role of the herders is periodically to drive the flocks back to centrally located control points for dipping, shearing, slaughter and so on. The

horses they use are among the most splendid working horses in the world, and it is not unusual to find a horse that spends part of its time out herding the sheep on the high karroo and the remainder of the year parading in the showring.

Heavy Horses
Herding horses are pleasant to ride: they have stamina, lightness of foot, and the ability to learn quickly. Thanks to their training in obedience to subtle commands, they are observant of the rider's needs and quick to respond to them – almost as if they were telepathic. It's no wonder, therefore, that they are tremendously popular among leisure-time riders and their popularity can be gauged by looking at a few statistics. In the United States, as a result of the radical transformation of techniques of agriculture and transport during the preceding decades, the total horse population had fallen in the 1920s from 11 million to 4 million. By 1959 the figure had sunk still lower, to 2.5 million . . . but by 1975 it had risen again to 9 million, and today it is not all that far short of the original figure. The Quarter-horse accounts for about one million of these animals: it may be the most numerous breed in the world.

Alongside this phenomenal rise in the number of horses being kept for pleasure there was a similarly phenomenal drop in the number of heavy working horses in use. Until a few years ago it was customary to say that the day of the heavy horses was done. That is no longer true; they have made an unexpected comeback, not only as ornaments of the showring but also fulfilling the tasks which they have carried out for centuries – pulling carts and wagons, lugging timber, and often, surprisingly enough, working under the plough.

In logging country all over the world these horses earn their keep by hauling the heavy lumber to the sawmill; while in many parts of the world the heavy horse can pull a load to places inaccessible to trucks and lorries. Among the more specialized uses of heavy horses are, in parts of Canada and New England, to bring loads of maple syrup from the depths of the forest to the processing plant, and, in other parts of the world, to pull brewers' drays and other similar

A trace of la gloire *is kept alive in Chad by the native Spahi mounted regiments.*

vehicles although, to be fair, the motive here is generally publicity rather than efficiency. The demand for heavy horses, for whatever purpose, is not a huge one but it is an insistent one, and good specimens can fetch high prices. In 1984, for example, it was thought worth while to export 63 Shire Horses from England to the United States.

Heavy horses were originally developed for war: they carried knights in armour. When the advent of firearms changed the nature of the battlefield, the horses were handed on from the master to his servants, to the people who worked his land for him so that he would have enough wealth to go to war. Heavy horses could thrive only where the soils were heavy and the fodder fat, but there they were of inestimable assistance in helping people wring a living from clayey and marshy soils. From the end of the eighteenth century, once a good road network had been built up in Europe, the heavy horses found a new sphere of employment in the transport of goods. When the internal-combustion engine came along, the numbers of heavy horses fell gradually and then precipitately: as an example, the stud-book of the Rhineland Heavy Draught Horse in 1948 held 27,000 horses, but by 1968 this number

had dropped to only 48! Some breeds of heavy horses became to all intents and purposes extinct; others remained only as showring horses – and then, as we have seen, the heavy horses made their almost miraculous comeback. Mind you, it is too early yet to judge whether this revival is a permanent thing.

Police Horses
The world's most famous mounted police force is undoubtedly the Royal Canadian Mounted Police (RCMP), originally formed in the northwestern regions of Canada. Since 1940, when the Mounties began to breed their own horses specifically for police work, their animals have been tall (16 hands or more), black or dark brown, and with a lot of Thoroughbred blood. The RCMP, alas, is a thing of the past so far as police-work is concerned, but the Mounties still perform in shows and tattoos, giving demonstrations of fine horsemanship.

Elsewhere in the world, most police forces have mounted units. In Britain there is the City of London Mounted Police, whose horses play a

Above, these Nigerian riders have come to celebrate the end of the fast of Ramadan.

Right, magnificently clad in adornments that are centuries old, this horse is greeting a state president in Chad.

prominent part in the annual Lord Mayor's Show parade. In London in general, police horses have rather less glamorous duties, notably in coping with demonstrations, where they can be used with considerable effect to split up large groups of civilians. They have played a similar role in other parts of the country in breaking up mass picketing. Their use in such contexts has occasionally been controversial. In the United States mounted police are seen only infrequently in the cities, and hardly more often outside them. The few police horses used tend to be rather smaller than in either Britain or Canada, and are of no particular breed, although Morgans are popular.

When you next see a police horse in the street, bear in mind that you are looking at an animal that has probably been more thoroughly trained

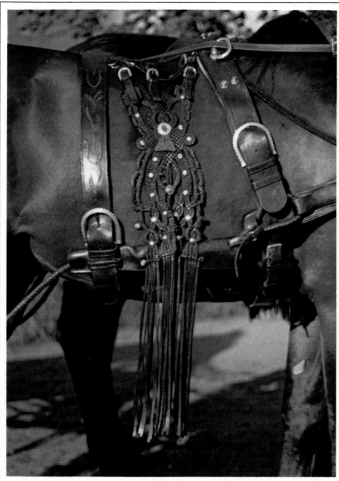

Left, the shalankas *that form part of the Hungarian harness are made with skill and artistry from leather and metal. Right, the traditional 'aprons' worn by the horses of the King of Morocco's stud are made from wool.*

than any other you will ever see. In these violent times, the life of its police rider may very well depend on the training which that horse has had.

Military Horses
Very few countries today possess cavalries, but most nations permit themselves a reminder of the past glories of mounted troops by retaining units of horse for ceremonial use. The crowds come to applaud; visiting dignitaries are impressed and flattered in a way they could never be by whole fleets of gleaming Rolls-Royces. But ceremonies such as Britain's annual Trooping the Colour are more than just tourist attractions: they symbolize a way of life which has perhaps gone for ever but whose ideals live on.

There is a lesson for the horse-lover to learn from such parades, too. Horses find it easier to be taught, and acquire the habit of obedience better, when they are raised and trained in the company

Top left, it took four men an hour to saddle up and decorate the sultan's Arab stallion. Top right, the strips on the headpiece are forged from silver Maria Theresa thalers. Bottom left, this Fulani warrior seems unconcerned as to whether or not his mount can actually see anything! Bottom right, a Japanese archer in traditional Samurai costume for the mounted archery contest called Yabusame. Their horses, too, are fitted out in ritual colours.

of others of their own kind. The hundreds of superbly groomed horses moving in perfect synchronism down a city street represent, in effect, an artificial herd. It cannot be stressed too often that horses are herding animals and, as such, incapable of realizing their full potential outside the context of the herd.

In parts of Africa cavalry armies are more than just symbolic or decorative, although this is rapidly changing. For example in Chad, a former French colony, a trace of the old *gloire* is kept alive in Spahi regiments, where native soldiers perpetuate French military regulations, French drill and French uniforms. You can see these proud and impressive black men on their black horses, riding easily and a little arrogantly in the manner of all desert riders, standing in the stirrups with the reins held high and the hands close behind the horse's neck. The lively little Sudanese horses hold their heads up and gallop like their cousins, the Arabs and Berbers, with their noses in the air and their hindquarters set low underneath.

Elsewhere in the Sahel one encounters mounted soldiers who seem to have been brought by time-machine straight from the Middle Ages. The Sahel is a belt of savanna, limited to the north by the Sahara and to the south by the Equator, which stretches right across Africa and embraces parts of the present-day states of Chad, Mauritania, Sudan, Cameroon, Nigeria, Niger, Mali, Burkina Faso, Benin and Senegal; it is an area bedevilled by droughts. Across the new and often arbitrarily drawn state boundaries the ancient tribal links still exist: the lenidos, sultans, emirs and caids still enjoy high respect and retain their own mounted armies of lifeguards.

Also of interest in the Sahel are the Fula, a cattle-breeding, hunting people of Hamitic origin who have since time immemorial kept large cavalry armies; and the Hausa, who have both Arab and Negro blood and who practise trade. For centuries these two peoples competed bloodily with each other in slave-hunting and -trading, fighting over trade routes and over plunder.

The animals which they bred were not clearly definable breeds but contained rather randomly

The American Morgan, standing about 14.1–15.2 hands, is an ideal horse both for leisure riding and for work.

mixed blood with strong infusions of local stock whenever the quest for booty took their masters into new territory. The Sudanese horses contain blood of the Berbers from North Africa, of the Arabs from the eastern end of the Sahel, and of the Galla and Dongola horses from Ethiopia (which themselves have Persian forebears), in varying proportions. Under the hard living conditions of this sub-Saharan belt, where the temperature variations are severe and where fodder becomes virtually nonexistent in times of drought, with poor treatment and often crazily reckless use, they have 'degenerated' into lean, tough little horses, no more than 13·1 hands high. But their performance is amazing.

In the last few years these cavalry horses have been eclipsed – as they probably will be for several years to come. The desert wars in the Sahel are being conducted with jeeps, tanks and lorries, and the horses have been confined largely to ceremonial use. More significantly, however, the area has been locked in the grip of extreme drought. Many of the horses of the Sahel cavalries have fulfilled the same function as the very earliest horses with which mankind came into contact. They have been used as a source of meat.

RACING

The Thoroughbred

During the sixteenth and seventeenth centuries, people on the continent of Europe were interested only in horses that were suitable for Haute École or coaching, creating breeds like the Lipizzaner, Frederiksborg and others. The British, however, concentrated almost to exclusion on the idea of breeding *fast* horses and racing them against each other along racetracks specially prepared for the purpose. Charles II had a race-course laid out at Newmarket and took to living there for part of the year; his presence, of course, drew the nobility like moths to a flame. A great deal of racing took place, and the breeding of ever-faster horses became intensive. British travellers brought back with them from the east Arab, Berber, Turkish and Persian stallions, and when these were crossed with home-bred mares they produced offspring which, with further careful breeding, became faster and faster with each succeeding generation.

The first edition of the *Racing Calendar* was published in 1727 by John Cheney, and this guide has appeared, either monthly or annually, ever since, making it possible to verify the individual successes of English Thoroughbreds anywhere in the world. And in 1793 this new breed, the Thoroughbred, became the first in the world to have its development accurately logged in the studbook, with the appearance of the *General English Studbook* (usually called 'Weatherby's' or 'The Book'); this register gives the extraction of all brood-mares and their foals. Soon afterwards the Thoroughbred studbook was closed, so that subsequently the only additions to it have been the offspring of those stallions and mares that had already been granted admission.

Towards the end of the eighteenth century the Thoroughbred began to be exported – to continental Europe, the Americas, Australia and the British colonies elsewhere. Along with the horses, the English racing system was exported, too. Today Thoroughbreds all over the world race under virtually the same conditions and, thanks to the fact that horses travel very well by air, individual animals can be moved easily about the globe to compete anywhere on Earth.

Thoroughbreds are truly royal animals: their blood is 'bluer' than that of many kings, because there hasn't been a *mésalliance* in their family tree for over 25 generations! They make up the most exclusive horse association in history, all being derived from just three stallions – the Byerley (or Byerly) Turk, the Darley Arabian and the Godolphin Arabian (brought to England in, respectively, 1680, 1702 and 1728) – and 49 mares from the Royal Stud. From these ancestors the modern Thoroughbred has inherited the two tasks of winning on the racetrack and breeding new generations of winners.

There are racetracks all over the world, from Italy to Japan, France to America, Germany to Australia and New Zealand. Many are complex structures incorporating stands that seat thousands of spectators, restaurants, boxes and enclosures, car parks with space for as many as 10,000 vehicles, and electronically controlled racing stalls. The setting may vary from one part of the world to another, but the fascination and the competitive urge are just the same. In Cameroon you can see exciting racing amid the desert sands on tracks staked out with posts, while in the United States horses are raced on dirt- or sand-tracks which can become a mudbath if it rains. In some countries there are even snow-tracks, where the silent hooves throw snow high in the air to cover the scene with a glorious flurry.

Although Thoroughbreds generally do not race on the flat during the winter months, there is winter racing at Seefeld, in the Austrian Tyrol and on the frozen lakes at Amora and St Moritz in Switzerland. In 1906 at St Moritz someone had the idea of using sleigh-horses to pull a skier instead of a sleigh, and soon people were skikijöring (see page 82) like this as well as flat-racing on the lake itself, which was frozen to a depth of about 18in (46 cm) and provided a large and really flat area for racing. Nowadays the ice-races

Racing on ice is a very popular winter sport in both Austria and Switzerland.

that are held in January and February are a firm favourite with the public – and even steeplechases have been held on the frozen lake. Naturally precautions are taken to ensure that the layer of ice will withstand the strain, especially in steeplechasing, and the horses have sharp studs screwed into their shoes to give them a sure grip on even the smoothest of surfaces.

At the Races

Thoroughbreds, apart from novices, do not generally race over short distances: that is the prerogative of the Quarter-horse. Flat races are generally run over distances of between 6 and 19 furlongs, with two-year-olds being raced over 4½-6 furlongs. Horses that specialize in short, fast races are called 'fliers'; those that do better in longer races are known as 'stayers'.

The classic distance is 1 mile 4 furlongs, and this is the length of the Derby, which takes place every June on the Epsom Downs in the south of England. The Derby is the most famous of the five English 'classic races' reserved for mares and entires (no geldings); the other four are the Oaks (1 mile 4 furlongs), the St Leger (1 mile 6 furlongs 132 yards), the Two Thousand Guineas (1 mile) and the One Thousand Guineas (1 mile). (All the distances given here are approximate. A furlong equals 201 m.) Only three-year-olds are allowed to take part in the classics, and the winner of the Derby is the absolute king – or queen – of the racing year.

Apart from the classic races, in which conditions are the same whatever the country in which the race is being run, the temperaments of the different nations play a decisive part in the detailed organization of their racing. For example, the French prefer middle distances – over 10 furlongs – and let their two-year-olds race only a very little; the English and Americans, on the other hand, like to get their horses fit early, and send them in for brisk, thrilling races of up to 7 furlongs. This very early use of the young Thoroughbreds is possible as a result of a number of factors – centuries-old selection for early readiness, special food and training, very light riders and so on – all determined by the economic constraints of horse-breeding, which has become a major industry. By contrast, no demands are made on elderly Thoroughbreds, many of which, if raced too long, would 'break down'; that is, develop problems in tendons, joints and bones.

Horses that are not fast enough on the flat can compete in hurdle races and steeplechases. In the latter the horses jump over massive hedges, fences and ditches, whereas in hurdle races they instead go over broom hurdles which must be 'skimmed' – that is, scraped over with the hind-legs. They need to maintain their tearing speed on the flat, but the momentary flight over the hurdles gives them a chance to catch their breath; a good jump can gain a horse several feet over the other runners.

Steeplechases (see page 108) are not run at the same rate as hurdle races and can therefore be longer – of distances generally between 2 and 4 miles (3–6½ km). The courses, which have wide bends over the jumps, are often found on the inside of the oval of a flat-racing track. The keenest enthusiasm for steeplechasing is largely confined to Britain and Ireland, where leading steeplechasers enjoy almost the same fame as their flat-racing counterparts. On the European mainland steeplechasing has generally been the sole province of army officers.

One of the peculiarities of flat-racing is that horses are ridden not by their owners but by jockeys. In the time of Charles II, boys were put on horses to reduce the weight the animals had to carry and thereby improve their chances of winning. The aristocratic owners of those days were far from calorie-conscious and, anyway, they found betting and spectating far less dangerous and perhaps even more fun than riding. Today's jockeys are usually feather-weight adults. So that horses can always meet each other on as equal terms as possible, there is a handicap system: complicated computations are carried out annually, taking into account the wins, placings and ages of the horses, so that the weight (including that of the jockey) which each horse must carry can be assessed.

Jockeys wear bright silks and caps in the colours of the owners of their mounts. The Romans used to give their charioteers six colours so that spectators could more easily follow the progress of the race. Each team would carry one of the colours green, red, white, blue, yellow and purple. Nowadays there are so many racehorse owners that the jockeys' colours have to be more

Quarter-horses, with their characteristically strong bodies and compact necks, racing over the quarter-mile course.

For racing on ice, the shoes of the horses must be fitted with studs to prevent them from slipping.

complicated than this, so that at the races you see a brilliant display of checks, stripes, dots and colour combinations.

Racing owes much of its popularity to the exhilaration of betting – and, as a sport, it is certainly far more suited than almost any other to give thrills and colour to gambling. You can watch the race progressing, enjoy the increasing tension as the runners shoot ahead or temporarily fall behind, allow your enthusiasm to come to boiling-point as the horses do battle down the home straight . . . and sometimes you can even win a little money. In the beginning, in the dazzling entourage of King Charles, prestige played its part in the excitement of betting, with courtiers keen to outdo each other with larger and

larger wagers, but nowadays most race-goers either gamble with a little money, just to make the racing more interesting, or approach the whole enterprise in the hope of making a profit.

The Quarter-horse

It would be a mistake to think that racing is confined to the Thoroughbred. Another very fast breed, the Quarter-horse, is run in highly prized races in the United States, Canada and Australia.

The Quarter-horse is of average size but has enormously broad quarters which provide the strength to propel the body forward like a rocket. By contrast with the Thoroughbred, this breed came about almost by chance; although its early members were carefully selected from good stock, they were bred with varying needs in mind.

For the first century following the discovery of the New World the only horses to be mated were those which had been imported from Spain.

However, the East Coast colonists, who maintained close contact with the mother country, England, began to bring in some top-class stallions of the then-new Thoroughbred and these, when crossed with native mares, produced a fast, powerful horse that satisfied all the settlers' needs. The inherent British passion for racing infected the New World, but the colonists had neither the time nor the money to build expensive racetracks or to keep horses exclusively for racing, and so they found a compromise: on Sundays they let their working horses race down the straight, unpaved streets of the townships or, sometimes, on a small track cleared in the nearby wilderness. For practical reasons a quarter of a mile (402 m) seemed to be a good race-distance, and it soon became clear what type of horse was

Below, racecourses the world over are always carefully tended, and their turf is specially treated to ensure good going.

Overleaf, horses and riders together face a tough assignment in the steeplechase.

most likely to win over it. In addition to having the characteristics discussed under rodeo-riding the ideal horse would have to be able to start like a bullet, and so would need muscle-packed hind-quarters. Breeding efforts were concentrated accordingly.

At the start of the nineteenth century the breed had become what was known as the 'Famous and Celebrated Colonial Quarter Panther', and it wasn't long before this turned into the earliest recognized breed of the United States, the Quarter-horse. Thanks to the pioneers, it soon spread from the East Coast all over the continent, although it was not until the 1950s that racing with Quarter-horses would get going on a grand scale in the western states.

Today there are many quarter-mile tracks and this form of racing is increasingly popular. In 1979 the Quarter-horse breed was able to boast the biggest prize in the whole preceding history of horse-racing: the winners of the All-American Futurity Stakes in that year shared a total 'pot' of $1,280,000.

Above, hurdlers need to have their legs well protected to avoid lacerations as they brush the fences.

Right, the excitement reaches fever pitch as the leading jockey does his best to hold off the challengers.

Horses for Trotting

There is another major category of racing horses: those that are bred for their speed not in the gallop but in pulling a small, light, two-wheeled single-seater carriage known as a sulky. The breeds which specialize in trotting races are, naturally, collectively called 'trotters'.

Trotters appeared in the eighteenth and nineteenth centuries in three different countries: Russia, France and North America. Road networks were improving, as was carriage-design, and riding at ease in a sulky was much more comfortable than sitting for long hours in the saddle. Soon the hunt was on to breed better and faster harness-horses.

In the case of Russia we know exactly how the

country's trotters came into being. Count Alexis Orlov, brother of one of Catherine the Great's lovers, was too big to be a rider – especially over the formidable distances between the capital and his estates in southern Russia. A clever man with a sensitive 'feel' for breeding, he set out to develop a better carriage-horse. His representatives – he had the advantage of wealth – went in search of a suitable oriental stallion as far as Greece, where in 1775 they purchased Smetanka, a grey Arab stallion.

Smetanka, bought for the unprecedented price of 60,000 roubles, sired the stallion Polkan I out of a Dutch mare. Polkan I's characteristics were not outstanding, but in 1784 Orlov put him to a Dutch Hartdraver mare, who produced a grey, Bars First, which became the father of the breed now called the Orlov Trotter. Bars First was a large, elegant, spirited horse with outstanding trotting abilities, and Orlov used him with mares which had similar characteristics – for example, an Arabian-Danish-Dutch crossbreed. By pursuing a carefully controlled policy of selective breeding,

Above, a group of competitors going down to the start of a trotting race. The horses are specially bred to the gait.

Right, trotting races are immensely popular in North America, and are held in all weather conditions.

Orlov developed what were the fastest trotting horses in the world at that time.

The first harness races were held in the Moscow winter of 1799, with light troikas or sledges being used. At the beginning of the nineteenth century the Orlov Trotter was known all over the world as both a racehorse and a carriage-horse. Orlov Trotters are still bred in Russia today, where they are both raced and used as working horses.

In North America the trotting horse was developed at about the same time as the Quarter-horse. Not all of the colonists' working horses were suitable for racing under the saddle, and not unnaturally those people whose domestic horses were normally used to pull carriages and traps

wanted to share in the excitement. The trotting race came into being.

The fastest working horses in America at that time were the Narragansett and the Canadian Pacer; these were crossed with imported English carriage-horses to produce animals which could amble in front of a cart or go at a broken trot under a rider. Two English Thoroughbred stallions – Messenger (imported in 1788) and his descendant Hambletonian – when crossed with local mares, produced improved trotters. Their

This horse seems scarcely to be touching the ground as it trots effortlessly along in the lead.

progeny became faster and faster, and were soon running on specially prepared racetracks.

To be accepted for racing, untried carriage-horses had to show that they could run a mile (1.6 km) within a certain time – that is, within a preset 'standard'. The breed therefore became known as the Standardbred. Moreover, there were two different types of Standardbred, according to the two different types of gait which came naturally to the horses. On the one hand there were the pacers, in which the two legs on the same side moved simultaneously, and on the other there were trotters, in which the diagonal pairs of legs moved together. The talent for the two different types of gait is very much a matter

Special harness has been put on the legs of these pacers to prevent them from breaking into a trot.

of heredity, and in the United States separate races are held for pacers and trotters; some horses are capable of running in either, but are not allowed to switch from pace to trot, or *vice versa*, in the course of a race. On average, pacing is a slightly faster means of progress than trotting, but the difference is small.

The American Standardbred is distinguished by its renowned good temper. It typically stands at 15·2 hands, is robust, muscular and powerful, and has a long frame.

The French Trotter is larger than its cousins but just as fast, and France is today one of the leading countries in the breeding and racing of trotters. Some of the most expensive trotting races in the world are held on the racecourses of Paris, and eager racegoers jet in from all parts of the globe. Something unique to France is that trotting races are sometimes held under saddle.

The breeding of trotting horses is significantly different from that of those for flat-racing. Trotters are mainly farm-bred, from mares which have ended their career as working horses and are now being used under the saddle for leisure riding. Until the 1930s it was quite common in Europe to see trotters pulling the butcher's or the baker's cart during the week and then competing at the local racetrack on Sunday. Things have changed a little, but there are still, in addition to the professional drivers and trainers, many amateurs, both men and women, involved in the sport. And, in contrast to most other types of sport, there are hardly any limits on age, weight or bodily build; the sulky, the light, four-feet-wide trap, is so designed that the driver's weight has virtually no effect on the horse's performance.

Until the 1930s trotters which were unsuited to the track or whose track-racing days were over were bought by tradespeople to serve as workhorses or even, in the country, as carriage-horses. The internal-combustion engine has spelled the end of such practices, but these horses can instead be retrained to move at a broken trot; this highly valued pace has different names around the world – in the United States alone, for example, it is known as the rack, Tennessee walk, flatfoot or singlefoot. It is a four-step pace, with the feet being set down separately one after the other in a clear 1-2-3-4-1-2-3-4 step. The rider is carried along comfortably, with little jolting.

The particularly well humoured character of the trotter, his great tolerance of the weather, his strong, sound bones and his overall robustness make him an ideal leisure companion. Although his body structure precludes him from dressage, he is otherwise one of the best, lightest-footed and most willing mounts.

Skikijöring

Wherever there is a lot of snow in winter, and the streets and paths are straight, you will find people enjoying the thrills of being pulled along on skis by a mounted rider. Skikijöring, done on ice, is rather different: it requires considerably more skill and involves a fair degree of danger. In skikijöring the horse has no rider, and so must be controlled by the skier by use of two long reins attached to the bit. The skier also has two traces which are fastened to the harness, and it is these which take the strain of pulling him along.

Skikijöring as a sport is found exclusively in the Seebahn area of Swiss St Moritz. It was first admitted into the official winter programme at St Moritz in 1923.

The excitement of skikijöring can begin before

In skikijöring (below, right and lower right), unlike skijöring, the horse has no rider, being guided solely by the skier behind. This sport can be very dangerous.

the race even starts, because getting the horses to the starting-line is by no means an easy business. The spirited Thoroughbreds have to be led there on long traces, and if they suddenly decide to gallop off towards the other side of the lake there is little the would-be racer can do to stop them.

That is the light-hearted aspect of the thrills of skikijöring. More seriously, the sport is dangerous enough to be a reasonably frequent killer. Until the advent of the vizored protective helmet, competitors could expect to suffer cut and bruised faces as compacted chunks of snow and ice were thrown back at high speed by the horses' hooves.

Moreover, while a competent skier can use traces long enough to ensure that the dangers from flying ice thrown back by his own horse are minimized, and likewise the risks of his horse's rear feet stamping on the tips of his skis, he has no control over what other competitors are doing. Inevitably there are collisions, or horses can accidentally tread on the skis of the competitors in front. Some types of accident can be worse; for example, one horse may run between another horse and its pursuing skier, tangling the traces and creating a situation that can be lethal to horses and skiers alike.

DRIVING

Nobody knows which came first, the riding of horses or the harnessing of them to pull vehicles. However, we do know with reasonable certainty that around the middle of the third millennium before Christ at least one culture, the Sumerians of Mesopotamia, had taken to using horses rather than onagers (wild donkeys) to draw their war-chariots. From the surviving pictures of these chariots we can see that they consisted of an underframe to which were attached both a fixed draw-shaft and a wooden or basketwork body in which the driver stood; the carriages could either be single-person vehicles or carry a second war-rior. Originally the axles turned with the big wooden wheels, but in due course this system gave way to one of fixed axles with moving spoked wheels. Early on, the rims and hubs of the wheels were made of wood, but later this was covered with iron and finally the wheels as a whole were made of this metal. Riding in these chariots must have been incredibly uncomfortable and it was probably quite a skill simply to control them – they certainly weren't designed for travel-lers – and their use was made even more difficult by the lack of any suitable harness designed to accommodate the anatomy of the horse. What the Sumerians did was to take the yoke of a zebu (native ox) and put it over the horse's neck – whereupon it immediately slipped back over the flat withers. Their solution to this problem was to secure the yoke with a strap that ran around the front of the horse's neck – which meant that, when the horse was running at full tilt, it was partially throttling itself!

Nevertheless, after these rather clumsy begin-nings the use of war-chariots persisted for millen-nia, even though their operations were necess-arily restricted to flat, dry terrain. The Romans, however, stopped it in its tracks: their legions were at their deadliest on foot. Nevertheless the Romans did enlarge and modify the chariot so that it became a transport vehicle, and in some versions one could even lie down and relax or doze the journey away. (They also retained the original chariot for sporting use.) In a way, it was inevitable that the Romans would make this development, for they were responsible for by far the best road system that the world had seen up until that time: they built good, durable roads throughout Italy and in many other parts of their empire, and maintained them thoroughly. All through the empire there were post stations where State-employed postillions, veterinary sur-geons and craftsmen were based. The roads had milestones showing the distance from Rome – hence the saying that 'all roads lead to Rome'. The whole gigantic system facilitated the adminis-tration of the State and, in particular, allowed the easy flow of State correspondence and officials.

In the eighth and early ninth centuries Char-lemagne passed along these roads on horseback and in carriages when he travelled to survey his domain, but soon afterwards, during the early Middle Ages, the roads became impassable be-cause nobody bothered to maintain them. For several hundred years there was a hiatus in the history of carriage-driving. Heavy carts pulled by horses or oxen made their slow way from place to place, but passenger conveyances were a thing of the past. In many places the roads, which in marshy districts were nothing but muddy tracks, could be used only in fine weather. When it was necessary to move large bodies of people around, for example, when the emperor and his vast entourage travelled from one palatinate to another, everybody who was able to do so went on horseback while the heavy wagons of the baggage-train, hauled by oxen, went ahead or followed along behind as a separate, slower-moving unit.

During the Renaissance and particularly the

Above right, *a smart coach and four being driven from the box in appropriate trace-harness.*

Below right, *a well turned-out team of Hungarian Lipizzaners – but they're going dangerously close to the cone.*

84

Baroque period, magnificent state coaches were built; they were designed not for cross-country travelling but for local court occasions, such as parades and ceremonial processions. Even when used in this limited way they were devilishly uncomfortable. Typical was the Viennese court; and it is of special interest to us since it bred its own carriage-horses at two State stud-farms, one at Kladrub on the Elbe, in what is now Czechoslovakia, and the other at Lipizza in modern Yugoslavia. These magnificent horses were trained to move in the slow, high-stepping parade gait – a superb movement which somehow manages to be simultaneously slow-moving and yet never tedious.

The invention and development of springs on which the carriage body could be suspended, together with the gradual reappearance of good roads, led to the coach becoming once again an increasingly popular mode of transport by the end of the seventeenth century. As time went on, vehicles were developed to suit all purposes, all temperaments, and all roads until the carriage reached a peak during the late nineteenth century, when there were so many different types available that it would be difficult to list them all. The parson and the doctor, the merchant and the farmer – anyone who wanted to get about more rapidly than by walking – drove one of the many special types of carriage. You can get some idea of the density of the traffic by considering that, around the turn of the century, there were no fewer than 300,000 horses working in London. At about the same time, an American Cassandra warned that, if things went on and the New York traffic continued to increase at the current rate, by about 1920 the entire city would be four feet deep in horse manure.

Almost at once, however, the carriage was virtually wiped out: first there was the 'golden age' of the railways, then came the automobile and finally, surprisingly soon afterwards, the aircraft cut the times of longer journeys to a tiny fraction. However, if there was no niche left for the carriage as a straightforward conveyance, during the 1920s and 1930s the new sport of carriage-driving was developed. The luxury teams of horses which had been pushed off the roads reestablished themselves on the tournament scene. Moreover, as a matter of pride, many businesses and country gentlemen retained their carriages and horses, many of their owners having themselves mastered the difficult art of driving them. Only after World War II was this tradition completely broken. It seemed then as if

the age of the horse-drawn carriage belonged very firmly to the past: only a few teams of ponies competing here and there for fun kept the tradition alive.

But keep it alive they did. It is almost impossible now to chart the revival of coaching and driving, although we can note that in Britain Gilbeys, the wine-merchants, and, at Buckingham Palace and Windsor Castle, the Royal Mews – who have always maintained and driven a fleet of coaches for ceremonial purposes – kept the image of the horse-drawn carriage firmly in the public eye. Outside Europe, too, there were a

Women excel in this sport, especially as elegance of turn-out can gain bonus marks.

number of countries where the tradition had always been more sociologically important and, presumably for that reason, had remained healthier through the decades when the horse-drawn vehicle was disappearing from the roads; one thinks of North America and South Africa.

Competition Driving

In 1969, the international association for equestrian sports – the Fédération Équestre Internationale (FEI) – adopted carriage-driving as a sport in its programme, and standard rules were introduced. Driving has yet to become an Olympic discipline, but there are meetings today at both national and international level. In 1970 the first European Carriage-driving Championships were held in Budapest, and in 1972 the first World Championships took place in Münster.

Different driving styles have evolved in different countries. For international competitions two have been formally adopted: the Hungarian style and the English style. The two are different

Overleaf, a competitor is called out to give an individual demonstration before the judge makes a final decision.

Above, *a four-horse team, collar-harnessed in the English style, trotting beautifully in unison.*

Below, *the same horses as in the upper picture, but today they are pulling a different coach for the rigours of the marathon.*

Right, *the marathon calls for precise judgement of speed, gait and distance for each section. The course consists of hairpin bends, steep ascents and descents, water crossings and sharp bends – all of which are designed to tax the skill and stamina of the competitors and their horses alike.*

because born out of different circumstances.

The Hungarians preferred speedy, light horses with tremendous stamina harnessed to light hunting carriages with large wheels. The Hungarian landscape is predominantly flat, and the broad roads there allowed them to assemble their horses in wide spans – typically in a team of five horses, with two abreast directly in front of the carriage and three abreast to lead the way. The appropriate equipment for this arrangement (even when the number of horses is reduced to four) consists of a trace-harness with double-ringed snaffles and a stock-whip. This arrangement is popular also in Spain.

The English tradition, by contrast, involves the harnessing of rather more stately horses to heavier carriages which often had to pass through narrow streets and among heavy traffic. The horses wear a collar harness and the bit used is chosen individually for each horse, depending upon which seems most suitable. The Dutch, Germans and Swiss generally drive in much the same way as the English.

In tournaments the style of driving is optional:

Above and right, every year at the Calgary Stampede there are races for the mobile kitchens of the ranges – the chuck-wagons. The wagon has to be loaded by four outriders and raced across the arena and back.

the judges are primarily concerned with the standard to which it is executed. However, they will be very finicky about this, paying strict attention even to such apparently extraneous details as the postillions and passengers.

Most of the traditional types of carriage and harness have survived and can be seen today. Most frequently in use is the one-horse unit, which is the easiest to drive and the least expensive. Also popular is the Tandem unit, which looks especially attractive but requires well trained horses: the two animals go one in front of the other, an arrangement that originated in England. There is a three-horse unit using the same sort of single-file (line-ahead) arrangement – the Randem – but this is rarely seen, being difficult to manage. In the carriage-and-pair the two horses are driven side-by-side; this is the most popular arrangement after the one-horse unit. Three-horse carriages, with the horses side-by-side, do exist but are nowadays found only in Russia, in the form of the troika; this arrangement used also to be seen on London's horse-drawn buses. The four-horse team is a traditional, elegant and powerful combination which demands considerable driving skill: here two pairs of horses run one in front of the other. Apart from the five-horse teams already mentioned, there are also arrangements of six, eight, ten, twelve or more horses harnessed in pairs, but these are usually seen only at shows.

Both European and World Championships take the form of multiple exercises ('combined training') in four categories, spread over three days: on the first day come the presentation and dressage sections, on the second the cross-country marathon, and on the third the obstacle-driving section. This last is a stern test of the suppleness and fitness of the horses (and humans) after the gruelling exertions of the previous day.

In the **presentation** section the teams stand before the judges and are looked over in detail. The bearing and clothing of the driver and passengers are judged, and both horses and carriage are examined to ensure that they are in first-class condition and well matched to each other. The harness is studied to check that it is of the right type, properly adjusted, and in good condition. Finally, the judges have to consider the *overall* impression of the entry.

The **dressage** exercises are performed in a rectangular area measuring 40 by 80 metres (about 45 by 90 yards). The teams have to execute voltes (circles) and serpentine manoeuvres, straight lines and figures-of-eight, driving at different speeds and using a variety of gaits but always moving smoothly, elegantly and obediently. The teams must also display how they can reverse, turn and stop.

On the second day of the contest the teams go out into the open country for the **marathon** section, a drive of between 12½ and 25 miles (20–40 km), depending upon the rules of the individual competition. Both the gaits and the times allowed for each section are precisely prescribed. The course itself uses roadways and country tracks as well as passing over meadows and fields and through narrow entrances; to make the competition more exciting there are also hairpin bends, precipitous ascents and descents, and

water crossings. The cross-country marathon challenges not only the skills of the driver but the stamina, condition and obedience of the horses.

The third day is taken up with **obstacle-driving**. Here red and white cones are used to define a course; the cones are freshly positioned for each carriage so that they allow a gap of only about 16 inches (40 cm) on either side of the wheel-hubs. The teams must negotiate the obstacle course fluently, knocking over as few cones as possible, since for each knocked over cone they lose penalty points. This wouldn't be too bad if the course was easy, but it isn't. The carriage must be backed into cul-de-sacs, driven over wooden bridges and around sharp curves as well as through water-obstacles – and, to make it worse, as quickly as possible, because the time taken counts towards the driver's score. As you can imagine, the drivers have to be virtuosos: they have two or four strong horses pressing forwards and only inches to play with on either side, yet they are allowed to convey instructions to the horses only by use of their voice, the reins and the tip of the whip. And all at breath-taking speed!

The Calgary Stampede
Each year since 1912 the Calgary Stampede has been held: it is one of the most famous horse festivals – if not *the* most famous – in the world.

Above, the skill of the chuck-wagon drivers is demonstrated as the teams turn the corner to race back.

Right, a charming little team. Eight Shetland ponies, two with foals at foot, are exhibited at a horse-show near Los Angeles.

The first meeting lasted four days and was attended by people from North America only; nowadays the festival lasts for 10 days and draws people from every part of the globe. They have come to see an orgy of rodeo-riding, with both saddled and unsaddled horses, steer-wrestling, brahma-bull riding, racing, and even the milking of wild cows. The most spectacular event of the Calgary Stampede is the chuck-wagon race.

The chuck-wagon is the mobile kitchen used on ranches: it goes with the cowboys out among the herds and on their weeks-long treks to the loading stations. It consists of a four-wheeled, low-slung box-wagon half-covered by a rounded canvas roof. The cooking equipment is carried in a square box at the rear, and there is a rear flap which serves as a kitchen table. Inside the wagon are cupboards and boxes containing all the things that might be needed on the journey but cannot be carried by the mounted cowboys – such as medicines and spare parts, ammunition and tools. Also inside are provisions for a month, as well as the cowboys' bed-rolls and spare clothing. Finally, there are two water-barrels slung on the sides, and hanging underneath is a buffalo-skin containing firewood gathered during each day's travel. The wagon is drawn by a team of four horses or mules; its absolute master is the cook.

In reality, out on the ranges, the chuck-wagon has changed over the years; but this description fits the vehicles used in the races at the Calgary Stampede. In each race there are four teams, made up of the wagon with its team of four horses as well as four mounted horsemen. They start at the narrow end of the large arena: each wagon stands with its rear flap lowered and the box containing the cooking equipment beside it. At the signal, the helpers throw the box into the back of the wagon and then swing up into their saddles which the 'cook' drives off at a full gallop. On reaching the far end of the arena the wagons must circumnavigate a water-butt before driving out onto the racetrack. The winner is the team which completes the half-mile (800 m) course first and having incurred the least number of penalty points. To give you some idea of how quickly all this happens, times of only a little over one minute are not uncommon.

The whole festival gets its name from the final stages of the chuck-wagon race, when the driving takes on all the characteristics of a stampede. Just as the half-wild herds of cattle used to run jostling and thundering for hours upon end after some trivial alarum had startled them, the horses and wagons in the race rush towards the finish in a completely uninhibited pell-mell frenzy.

The Goodwood Show
At the opposite extreme from the wild turmoil of the Calgary Stampede is the Goodwood Show, held annually near Cape Town in South Africa.

The first Dutch settlers brought with them their splendid teams of Dutch Friesians, and in later years imported more. One way in which the wealthy were able to show off their status was by having magnificent teams of horses, and it is this tradition which still thrives at the Goodwood Show today. One interesting point is that the people involved in the show are most typically to be seen wearing their everyday working clothes:

Overleaf, *the driving of this team at South Africa's annual Goodwood Show is a four-man effort.*

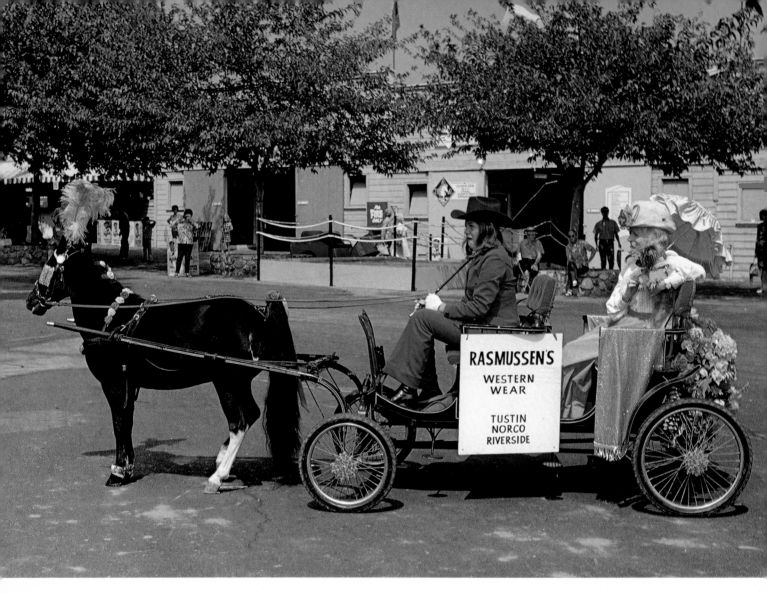

This bright turn-out has an air of carnival gaiety . . . almost despite the fact that its motives are for publicity.

the splendour of the spectacle is concentrated on the horses.

'Splendour' is not too grand a word to use. Over 1000 horses take part. They are uniformly dark, but their harnesses are snow-white. The carriages, which vary in type according to the class, are painted green and red with white edgings, and are often decorated with painted floral motifs. Horses and carriages together represent an ostentatious display of wealth – *real* wealth.

Unlike Calgary, there are no competitive races at the Goodwood Show, and unlike the European tournaments there are no prescribed exercises. The teams are presented in whatever manner the driver has decided is best. The judges examine gaits and temperament, the absolute precision of the gait, and the obedience and attractiveness of each team, the horses of which should be as near as possible exactly the same size. The driving is done both on an oval half-mile (800 m) track and on the grassed area enclosed by it. The drivers make their teams perform the tightest figures-of-eight, curves and arcs as fast as they possibly can;

all the time they are up against the pressures of competition and driving within an inch of disaster. It is a fantastic demonstration of obedience, speed and agility on the part of the horses – and consummate skill on the part of the drivers.

The show really gets off the ground with the appearance of the eight-horse teams: eight high-spirited horses pull a long country wagon at full gallop across the arena and then around the track. The excitement becomes intense as maybe eight or nine teams take part together, the spinning wheels of the wagons coming within inches of each other as they juggle for position. Each team has at least five people involved in the driving: three or more hold the reins, one uses the whip, and one is stretched out on the floor feverishly cranking the brake on the rear wheels. In addition, there are passengers clinging to the wagon's boards, holding on for dear life as the vehicle is thrown about all over the place.

Promenades and Parades
Although most of this chapter is concerned with competitive carriage-driving, the vast majority of the driving done in the world is not for competition at all, but for pleasure and/or display. It would be impossible even to estimate the numbers of carriages in the world which are used for

nothing more gruelling than a quiet drive in the country. In the British Isles such carriages are nowadays a very rare sight indeed – less so in Ireland – but in some parts of the European mainland they are not so uncommon.

In Britain and the Netherlands another form of carriage-driving continues a long-standing tradition: elegant teams on parade in small-scale Sunday shows.

Carriage-driving in the Netherlands goes back a very long way. Centuries ago the farmers and merchants used to drive their high-wheeled carriages across the country's broad, flat expanses: on Sundays they would be going to church and on weekdays they might be going to market . . . in either case, impromptu races were not uncommon. The rapid trotting horses they used, of Friesian or related stock, have made major contributions to the blood of various trotting breeds now used for racing all over the world; and today the Friesian itself is regarded as a valuable horse in its own right, both for competitions and for leisure-time riding or driving. Many people in the Netherlands derive great pleasure from seeking out old Friesian carriages, renovating them with loving care and patience, and then showing them off to fellow enthusiasts and the general public in local shows. Often enough, the passengers will be dressed in traditional costume, just to make the display that much more charming.

Another carriage-horse, the Hackney, is much loved on both sides of the English Channel; it has a distinctive way of lifting its legs extremely high.

In both countries, people enjoy harnessing and parading ponies. This is a hobby which is not too prohibitively expensive, but it does involve a fair amount of time, dedication and knowledge, because it is no easier to drive a small horse well than it is a big one. The range of carriage-types available for these small horses is far greater than you might think, because aesthetic and practical considerations dictate that the carriage has to be matched to the size of the horse. The horses, carriages and passengers are all rigged out in the most decorative way, and the combination which is most attractive may win a prize – if there are prizes to be won. Many of the teams have a theatrical touch. You can see gypsy caravans complete with authentic-looking gypsies; dog-carts complete with a 'governess' and her 'pupils' all dressed in turn-of-the-century style; wedding coaches with bridal pairs (in many parts of Britain such coaches are becoming increasingly popular for carrying real brides and grooms away from the church); and fully laden post-coaches with coach-men on the box. There seem to be no limits to the devotees' imaginations!

In many parts of the world it is not uncommon to see carriages still being driven for purposes of publicity or advertising. One of the illustrations shows an attractive horse and carriage discovered by the photographer in California. This carriage was taking part in a fair near Los Angeles which featured a mixture of races and horse-sales, a menagerie, an automobile exhibition, round-abouts and stalls – something for everybody, but a million miles from the spectacle of, say, the Goodwood Show. Also present was an eight-horse team of Shetland ponies, some of which had foals at foot who would take advantage of any pause in the proceedings to seek refreshment from their harnessed dams. Nobody could have failed to be completely captivated by these superbly turned out, intelligent little creatures.

Of all the uses to which horses are put by mankind, carriage-driving is probably the one which is the kindest to the horse. No single animal has too much work to do and, working in a team, the horses have the reassurance of the presence of others of their own kind. It is therefore a particular pleasure to notice that the art of driving, after the decades of uncertainty, seems to be becoming more and more popular with each passing year. And, from a selfish point of view, we are able to enjoy watching some of the most elegant and graceful horsemanship anywhere in the world.

The little ones cannot be left at home while their mothers compete at the show!

HUNTING

It was only in comparatively recent times that hunting became a sport; before then it had been a means of survival. Early man hunted on foot for animals which would furnish him with meat and skins, and at some stage dogs became involved in this. Later on mankind tamed the horse to assist him in hunting, but at what stage these three elements were combined to form a single unit that could hunt more efficiently than before we simply do not know.

At the end of the thirteenth century Marco Polo described the great hunting expeditions which he had witnessed at the court of Kublai Khan. Just as they had for millennia on the steppes of central Asia, hundreds of huntsmen and thousands of beaters worked together in hunts that could go on for weeks on end. The purpose of these expeditions was threefold: to supply the tribes with adequate stocks of meat; to provide exciting entertainment for guests, friends and visiting princes; and to give the younger soldiers experience of discipline and the use of weapons.

Well over 1500 years earlier Xenophon had had the same view of hunting: 'It is particularly good practice for war,' he wrote, and devoted a chapter to it in his treatise on horsemanship. And hunting for sport – really for reasons of pomp – is depicted on a Persian Sassanid-dynasty silver vessel which still survives. The decoration shows the fourth-century King Shapur II galloping saddleless on a richly caparisoned horse: he is performing the difficult feat of twisting around to shoot an arrow into a lion behind him. He was not only demonstrating his horsemanship, he was displaying his royal status, for only the king was allowed to hunt lions.

Hunting had, therefore, a diversity of purposes, from the killing of meat to the ostentation of kings. It also had a great deal to do with the way of life of certain peoples. To the Plains Indians of North America it was a central part of life: they hunted because hunting was their only source of meat and skins. The buffalo figured largely in their mythology and legends because

from it came virtually all the necessities of life, and without it the whole culture would have collapsed. In Europe during the Middle Ages both aristocracy and peasants were obliged to hunt for the wild boar and deer which infested the extensive, thick forests of those days. Not only were they seeking food, they were attempting to protect their estates and crops from the ravages of these animals. In the Baroque period the rights of the peasantry were subjugated to those of the aristocracy, as the court took it as its privilege to hunt game wherever it led them, even through planted fields.

Sometimes the prey could be dangerous, if we are to believe the thirteenth-century Italian hagiologist Jacobus de Voragine. Long after his death his *Golden Legend*, a collection of lives of the saints, was translated into English and brought to Britain the tale of a Cappadocian ex-army officer and tax-collector called George, who went on horseback to fight a dragon. Athough this story was obviously a fable – and, in fact, Voragine muddled together the histories of at least three early Christians called George to produce a glorious portmanteau version – St George quickly became the patron saint of England, Portugal, chivalry, and riders everywhere.

Over the centuries one practical reason after another for mounted hunting disappeared: the dragon died out, meat was produced on the farms in sufficient quantities to feed at least the rich, and men did their training for war on the parade-ground rather than in the chase. In England great tracts of land had already, by the middle of the seventeenth century, become so deforested that the red deer had withdrawn into the mountainous regions of the north where hunting on horseback was almost impossible. In mainland Europe, by the end of the eighteenth century, the numbers of stags, does and wild boar had in

A meet of the Dungarvon Harriers in the courtyard of the fifteenth-century Bunratty Castle in Southern Ireland.

An Irish heavy-hunter, of a breed in demand the world over, clipped up and plaited out Irish-style, ready for action.

many areas become so catastrophically reduced by the systematic hunting of feudal and later times that there was really nothing left to hunt. And so people looked around for another animal to use as prey.

To Hunt the Fox
The animal that could still be found everywhere was the fox. In the Middle Ages the fox had been regarded as a simple menace which the farmer put down as best he could, but now the animal was elected to fill the role of a sly, cunning partner in a great game. The fox was not chosen for any practical purposes but simply because hunting it provided good sport, not least because it was cunning enough to outwit the hounds by retracing its steps or going to ground.

The motives of people who hunt are compara-
tively simple, and have nothing to do with practicalities. As many will admit, any useful benefits that accrue from their sport are merely secondary. What people wanted – and still want – was the thrill of the chase, the invigoration of the open air, and the daredevil pleasures of doing something rather dangerous. Where foxes are not to be found people will hunt other animals: hares are popular in many parts of Europe, while coyotes (as well as foxes) are hunted in some parts of the United States, jackals in India, and kangaroos in Australia (where foxes are also specially imported for hunting, particularly now that killing kangaroos is limited).

What the fox lacked in charisma compared with the stag, he more than made up for in other ways, especially since the nature of hunting was changing in accordance with the changing nature of the countryside. England, for example, by the end of the eighteenth century no longer had vast expanses of open country. If you wanted to chase the fox you now had to jump over a constantly

increasing number of hedges, fences, walls and ditches. Hunting might have lost all its practical purposes, but it had become the most exciting of all horseback games.

The Hunter's Paradise
England is still *the* classic hunting country, and some hundreds of packs are still kept there.

Above, *an Irish stud-groom with his charge, a Thoroughbred stallion brought in from the field to cover a mare.*

Below, *Irish Draught mares. These will produce a wonderful cross if put to a Thoroughbred stallion.*

Overleaf, *the huntsman casts his hounds in a typical Irish landscape with dry stone walls on all sides.*

A drag-hunt field, without a sign of hesitation, approaching a nice little hunt-jump.

However, the true paradise of modern hunting is in a different part of the British Isles – Ireland.

Here the sport was born not from feudal traditions but from a deeply rooted native affection for the horse. The horse is 'in the blood' of Irishmen of all walks of life. Perhaps this is because, in the mild climate created by the Gulf Stream washing against Ireland's west coast and on the country's chalky soil, the horse develops better there than anywhere else in the world. Also, Ireland largely escaped the Industrial Revolution: while everywhere else in Europe, from the nineteenth century onwards, the countryside was covered with an ever denser network of roads, canals and railways, and while automobiles, trucks and tractors ruthlessly replaced the horse, in Ireland large tracts of land remained completely undisturbed. The farmer continued to work the fields with his heavy horses, and the breeding of hunters became good business, especially if they had already been broken in by actual experience of hunting. The sport therefore became a part of the national economy and the fact that it gave such a lot of fun to everyone involved did it no harm at all. Unlike the case in the rest of the British Isles, therefore, in Ireland there has never been a groundswell of public opinion against hunting. Breeders and grooms, farmers and lords, lawyers and fishmongers, townspeople and children all came together, as they still do, to hunt.

For Irish fox-hunting your horse needs to have been familiar with the peculiarities of the terrain since its youth, for this is the most difficult hunting country in the world. A child on a Connemara pony once summed this up for the author: 'You don't have to be afraid. The ponies know the jumps, so all you must do is stay on top.'

The classic Irish hunter is not a single breed: two related crossbreeds collectively make up the grouping, both descended from the Irish Draught Horse. Unlikely as it may seem, these heavy animals, best known for pulling carts and working the land, are in fact enthusiastic jumpers. When an Irish Draught mare is covered by a Thoroughbred stallion the result is a heavyweight hunter of a type in great demand throughout the world. Even-tempered and with a powerful ground-covering gallop, full of the skill of self-preservation over the jumps, this is a horse for keen hunting men who are, shall we say, no longer lightweights in the saddle. The other type of hunter is produced by having mares from this first cross covered again by a Thoroughbred: the result this time is a lighter-quality hunter that is equally sought after.

Any discussion of the horses used in Irish hunting would be incomplete without mention of the Connemara Pony. Although these are only up to about 14 hands high, they are tough and well able to hold their own over all the obstacles, and make an excellent cross.

Such horses and ponies are bred mainly in western Ireland. Here they are at their best for hunting: they know every wall and every inch of ground because this is the territory on which they were reared. In agricultural terms the terrain is poor, the soil either stony or boggy – too hard or too soft for the successful growing of crops. And the most striking feature of the area is that it is criss-crossed by thousands upon thousands of stone walls. These drystone dykes go back centuries: from time immemorial they have been built by farmers simply picking up the stones that litter the ground and piling them up to define small fields.

In Ireland you either jump or stay at home. One Master of a pack of hare-hounds explained to the author: 'Less than 200 jumps in an afternoon and it's not a successful hunt.' In most parts of the world you're lucky to get 30! Yet it's not just a question of having numerous obstacles: to be really exciting they have to contain a certain element of surprise, something to set the blood coursing through your veins as you discover to your mild astonishment that you've survived.

In Ireland it's not at all uncommon to gallop at full tilt up to a three-foot wall and jump it before noticing that on the other side the tumbled stones of an earlier wall extend a further six feet or more – partly concealed with overgrowing brambles! Or, in the dim light of a winter's day, you may be riding along when your horse suddenly jumps over what appears to be nothing at all; looking back as the hooves touch the tarmac you realize that you've just cleared a wire fence. It was completely invisible to you, but mercifully your mount's keen eyes picked it up in the gloom.

In the west of Ireland the prey are mainly hares. Harriers, smaller than foxhounds and specially bred for the job, follow the scent. As there are a great many hares and their tracks criss-cross all over the place, the hounds have to make snap decisions as to which is the right one to follow. The horses go along with this: they slew themselves around without warning, perhaps unexpectedly jumping right-handed over a wall when the rider had prepared himself for a jump straight on. It's not easy keeping your seat in these circumstances!

On the eastern side of Ireland the hunting is different. Here the fields stretch out endlessly before you. They are not stony, and the walls so prevalent in the west are absent. Instead, the meadows and fields are bounded by broad, deep ditches at the side of which the soil has been built up to form banks. As you might expect, trees and bushes grow freely on the banks. Often enough, the neighbour on the other side has made a ditch in the same way, so that, when out hunting, you often have to jump a wide rain-filled ditch, land on a treeless part of the bank, and immediately jump off again to clear the ditch on the other side. To do this you need fast, sure-footed local horses with plenty of courage. This is where the famous Irish Hunter comes into its own.

Hunting Around the World

It's different in other countries. In Germany, Switzerland, Austria and elsewhere to hunt a living animal is not permitted. Instead one must opt for drag-hunting. A course perhaps five to 20 miles (8–32 km) long is picked in advance and provides a good number of obstacles. In the past, a lead rider would drag a moistened tow-ball along behind him, but in modern times he trickles a strong-smelling fluid from a canister. Trained to recognize this chemical, the hounds set off along the trail with the riders following behind. Of course, this is not really hunting at all, but it can be very good sport.

The bloodless nature of European hunting is not just a result of the increasingly widespread feeling that killing foxes and hares for sport is immoral. It has more to do with the fact that nowadays free hunting is virtually impossible, what with the closely built-up areas and densely proliferating road network on the European mainland. Even drag-hunting is uncommon these days: there are perhaps as many as 250 packs of hounds in England, but at the last count there were only 10 in all of Germany.

Every hunt is held according to strict time-honoured rules and regulations: no other equestrian sport can look back on such a long and eventful period of development. The recognized jargon is made up of a mixture of French and British terms, partially translated into the local tongues. The dogs are called hounds (foxhounds or staghounds) and do not run all over the place but in a pack. They are counted not as individuals but as couples – i.e. two hounds; during exercise training the young entry and experienced hounds are coupled together. If the hounds find a scent and remain on it, they produce a characteristically shrill hunting call, their 'cry'.

The beloved scarlet coat of the huntsman represents an old tradition with a meaning behind it. It really comes into its own only after the rain and the winter sun of many hunting seasons have bleached it to a pinkish-violet colour. It was originally worn so that riders who lost their way in unfamiliar countryside, or who fell and lay injured, could be found more easily.

Huntsman and hounds lead the field to draw the next covert. Strictly, the hounds should be bunched around the huntsman.

Steeplechasing

After five months of intensive hunting the horses were so fit that it seemed a crying shame to put them out to grass immediately. Their muscles were hard and taut, their legs were like iron, they could hardly be matched for strength and endurance. Moreover, their riders were also on top form. Someone came up with the idea of letting the horses race against each other across terrain similar to that of the hunt, straight from one landmark to another. The most obvious landmarks in those days were church steeples; hence the name. Modern steeplechasing has become a race over a predetermined track which is spotted with heavy obstacles; it is run under what are known as National Hunt rules.

In England, Ireland and the United States point-to-point meetings, run by individual hunts mainly for fund-raising purposes, are held at the end of the hunting season. They are for amateur riders on horses that have 'qualified' – that is, have gone to hounds a certain number of times.

The most difficult and certainly the most famous steeplechase in the world is the Grand National, held at Aintree, near Liverpool; it has been run on this track since 1839. The course is 4 miles and 856 yards (7200 m) long, and of the 16 obstacles 14 have to be covered twice, making 30 murderous jumps in all. A few statistics selected at random point up the difficulty of the race. In 1961, 35 horses started but only 14 of them finished the course. Fifteen years earlier, in 1946, only 6 finished out of the 34 that took part. And in 1928, although 42 horses started, only *one* finished uninjured and still with its rider in the saddle!

SHOW-JUMPING, EVENTING AND DRESSAGE

For a long time it has been debated whether or not horses enjoy jumping. Certainly in the wild they will go to great lengths to avoid having to jump over obstacles; but by contrast modern horses which have been specially selected and bred for jumping will quite often leap over a fence or a gate out of sheer enjoyment. Horses are very adaptable creatures: after they have been sufficiently trained to do something they will end up doing it for pleasure, even if it is directly contrary to their instinctive natures.

Saddles for Jumping

Throughout the centuries the most popular designs of saddles have featured very high front pieces and a split at the back: it would be very difficult to stay mounted in such a saddle during anything more than a simple hop. Modern cowboys in North America have saddles built along these general lines, and they make a point of avoiding having to jump obstacles. Of course, any cross-country rider will have to cope with leaping over a fallen tree-trunk or a narrow stream from time to time, but that is rather different. When seventeenth-century princes went hunting, they did so on wide pathways where countless generations of earlier riders had prepared the way for them: they owned the forests, after all, and so could ensure that matters were arranged just exactly as they wanted them.

Sociological changes, in terms of status and property, brought with them changes in the nature of hunting, and horse-jumping began to grow into what was almost a sport in its own right. Even so, the walls and fences that surrounded fields and orchards in those days were rarely more than about three feet (1 m) in height. In order to jump these, riders would use a method that seems very odd to us today: they would stick their feet out to the front and lean their bodies backwards, so that they were relying almost solely on the bridle for control of the horse's direction. It was also quite impossible for them to see where they were going, although this

didn't matter much because they could rely upon the horse to find its own way through the familiar terrain. All the rider really had to do was to stay on the horse's back.

Although this position was hardly conducive to high-jumping, the use of it did bring about an important change in attitudes. The control over the horse that it allowed was precarious at best, and this led people to realize that, when jumping at least, it was not necessary for the rider always to exercise complete control over his mount. Even today the English, Irish and North Americans, all of whom inherited this style, allow their horses considerable scope to exercise their own initiative, even if otherwise the riding styles they use are rather different.

Around the end of the last century a development in racing occurred in England which was to have profound implications for the evolution of the modern saddle. Before that time jockeys would sit in their long-stirruped saddles throughout flat races, and take jumps in much the same way as would their hunting fellows; but in 1897 an American jockey called James Todhunter (Tod) Sloan shortened his stirrups drastically so that he was riding above, rather than on, his horse. The English thought this was hilarious, and promptly dubbed the style the 'monkey-seat'; they certainly didn't realize that they were witnessing one of the most profound developments in horsemanship to have occurred for as long as 2000 years. Their laughter grew a little uneasy as the best English jockeys, riding the best horses, lost to Tod Sloan time after time. Finally the trainers took the trouble to analyse Sloan's new seat, and they realized that the secret of his success was that he was bringing more of his weight onto the front part of the horse, and thus reducing the load on the rear. This was important, for the horse's propulsive power comes from its hindquarters, its forelegs being used only for steering and control; removing the weight from the rear therefore allowed the horse to run faster. It was as simple as that. Almost overnight, the jockeys of England

Above, *Bruce Davidson of the USA on J. J. Babu at Badminton in 1985 shows how easy it can all look.*

Right, *another competitor at Badminton in 1985, Mrs Torrance Fleischmann on Finvarra.*

converted to the 'monkey-seat'; the French, Germans and Italians soon followed suit, and now the position is more or less standard for jockeys throughout the world.

Generally speaking, horses will jump over obstacles only if they have to, and so the role of mankind in the whole exercise is to make things as easy as possible for the horse. An important historical figure in this context was a young cavalry officer called Federico Caprilli, who in the latter part of the last century took a careful look at horse-jumping. Clearly, on the modern battle-field, the cavalry was a spent weapon; but cavalry horses (and riders) could be useful for reconnais-sance work, as they could travel at great speed over the countryside. It made good sense, there-fore, to train cavalry mounts not on the artificial parade-ground but in a natural environment. When his ideas were combined with the new notions of the racing seat, a completely new style of riding for horse-jumping emerged. The horse-man used short stirrups and sat well towards the front of the horse; and his hands were held wide and above the horse's shoulders, so that his mount's head, neck and back were free.

A Modern Sport

Showjumping came into existence as a sport at about the beginning of this century, and is therefore at least 1000 years younger than, for example, racing. Its beginnings were minor indeed. Old photographs survive showing the scene as it was at the very start. Typically a few military officers would jump over obstacles made from poles, perhaps three feet (1 m) high, scat-tered in the corner of a racecourse or training area, while the ladies would look on from the comfort of their carriages. A far cry from the modern showjumping arena.

Showjumping was in those days the domain of army officers, and would remain so for some time. When it was welcomed as a comprehensive discipline at the 1912 Olympic Games it was reserved exclusively for the military officers. Forty years would have to pass before women and army subalterns were allowed to take part in the Helsinki dressage event, where Lis Hartel of Denmark marked the occasion by taking a silver medal. And it was as late as 1956 that women

Left, *the smile says it all: Virginia Holgate with Priceless at the Badminton Trials in 1985.*

Above, *Conrad Holmfeld of the USA on Abdullah at the Los Angeles Olympics in 1984: they took the individual silver.*

were allowed to compete in the Olympic show-jumping at Stockholm (the equestrian events were held there rather than in Melbourne, with the rest of the Games, because of Australian quarantine laws); Pat Smythe was in the British team which took the bronze medal.

In the early days the sport was dominated by the Swedes, and then the period following World War I saw the rise of the Italian school. Since then the Poles, Germans, Swiss, Spaniards, Mexicans, English and French have all had their moments of glory. In recent years the United States, training under Bill Steinkraus and especially the Hungarian-born Bertalan de Nemethy, have risen from strength to strength, taking the gold medals for both team and individual showjumping (Joe Fargis) as well as the team gold in the three-day event at the 1984 Los Angeles Olympics.

While this form of horsemanship was probably at its most elegant during the period when it involved only the military, it would be wrong to think that its modern form did not contain a strong input from civilians. All over the Western world, especially in West Germany, Switzerland, Holland, England, France and Belgium, gymkhanas were held in their thousands: riding clubs with their own stables, arenas and outdoor facilities sprang up like weeds. And the favourite mounted activity became showjumping.

Better horses for this sport were developed in the traditional horse-breeding countries, namely England, Ireland and West Germany. Initially, the heavier local breeds were mated with Thoroughbreds to produce a better, more refined horse; sometimes Arabs were used to produce lighter and faster animals, but these were also more temperamental and consequently more difficult to handle. The best of today's jumping horses appear to be as eager as their riders to win, and quite obviously enjoy jumping. There is certainly no need to force them over obstacles.

However, showjumping does present dangers to the horses. This is not just because every sport will gather about it a few ruthless people who

simply don't care what damage they do so long as they win, but because there is a depressing tendency to introduce horses to showjumping while they are still too young. Jumping wears them out quickly, finally, and in great numbers. Horses that are still immature are given just enough training to allow them to master the mechanics of the operation but not any of the important points of technique, and are then expected to jump obstacles of six feet (1.8 m) or more. Leg damage, not unexpectedly, sets in by the time they are seven years old – the very age at which they ought to be becoming physically mature enough to take up jumping for the first time. One can only hope that people will learn to be less impatient.

Showjumping had already become a fairly highly developed sport by the time it became necessary to create strict rules to govern it. Initially all the nations who sent teams to the Olympics compiled their own rule-books, which were then combined to form the *Règlement Général*

Left, *Karen Stives on Ben Arthur at the 1984 Olympics, where she took the individual silver in the three-day event.*

Below, *Joe Fargis on Touch of Class at the 1984 Olympics: he won the team and individual showjumping gold medals.*

of the senior international equestrian organiz-ation, the Fédération Équestre Internationale (FEI). All equestrian tests are defined in terms of various categories: 'A' is for Beginners, 'L' means Easy, 'M' means Intermediate and 'S' means Difficult. Courses are set within these categories, and in each case the object is to go round the course as quickly as possible and without commit-ting any faults.

Showjumping competitions can be run either (a) against the clock, so that the person who finishes in the least time and with the least number of faults wins (there are, of course, complicated time–fault calculations), or (b) by an elimination process, whereby the people with the least number of faults at the end of the first round go through to the second, and so on. There is also a form of the sport in which the concentration is purely on the size of the jumps: there is no time limit, but with each round the jumps get bigger and fewer, so that the final round may involve only two jumps – but huge ones.

Besides the standard competitions, there are a number of interesting variants. In two-horse con-tests the rider performs the first part of the course on one mount and then switches to another, held waiting for him by an assistant. Since time is of the essence, the swap-over must be as swift as possible, and this demands considerable physical

skill on the part of the rider and cooperation from his mounts. In lucky-jump contests, treasure hunts, optional jumping and other forms of the sport, it is mostly up to the horseman to decide which obstacles he wants to go for within a particular set time; here the riders can accumulate points with every obstacle they successfully cross. Such events are very popular with the spectators.

In recent years the height of the obstacles has been a matter of some debate. For a while, during the 1970s, it seemed there was a trend to build ever bigger jumps, which gave an unfair advantage to the more powerful jumping horses such as those from Germany, and took away much of the accent from straightforward skill. Luckily, in recent years this trend has been reversed, and speed and ability have become the important features of the successful showjumper. Breathtaking speed and spot-on jumping accuracy are what will win the contest, not brute strength.

Eventing: The Military Connection
In the eighteenth century Frederick II of Prussia realized that his cavalry had to change if it was to be of any use on the modern battlefield: in brief, the regiments of horse had to be more mobile. He entrusted the task of reorganization to a cavalry general called Friedrich Wilhelm von Seidlitz. Von Seidlitz determined that there were three qualities in the ideal cavalry horse: (a) speed; (b) obedience, and control by the rider to the extent that the horse could be turned in its own length; and (c) reliability in the field, so that fences and ditches could be crossed without hesitation. By the time the cavalry as a war force ceased to exist,

Below, *Sue Pountain on Ned Kelly, winner of the Queen Elizabeth Cup at the Royal International Horse Show in Birmingham, 1985.*

Right, *Malcolm Pyrah winning the King George V Gold Cup at the 1985 Royal International Horse Show on Towerlands Anglezarke.*

some 150 years later, these aims had been modified, but only a little. Different training methods had been developed, dressage and jumping styles had changed, and in general sights were being set higher. In all these activities the traditional cavalry horse could now be surpassed by sporting types. Still, when in 1912 three-day eventing, the sport which embodied all of von Seidlitz's aims, was incorporated into the Olympics, the only people allowed to take part were military officers on service horses.

Horse Trials Today

From such origins among the cavalry the sport of eventing developed. In what are called either three-day events or horse trials, riders and their mounts are required to display excellence at dressage, cross-country riding and showjumping. As with many sports, the exact order of proceedings is not hard and fast, but generally dressage takes place on day one, cross-country on day two, and showjumping on day three. In fact, the expression 'cross-country' is used rather loosely here; the tests on day two are designed to test speed and endurance, and involve an initial section on roads at a trot or slow canter, a steeplechase, another road section, and finally a cross-country course. Certain standards are set for the individual degrees of difficulty, but the organizers can vary some of the dressage movements, alter the length of the course, and have individually designed courses for the steeplechase and cross-country race. The following description is of a typical Olympic three-day event.

Day one is devoted to dressage. The test involves 20 individual movements done from memory in a time of 7½ minutes, performed in the dressage arena, which has the dimensions 20 × 60 m (21·8 × 65·6 yards). The thing of interest in this section is not just the precision of the movements but the style. The rider has to show that the horse will follow his lead willingly and obediently; that it can be effortlessly accelerated and decelerated; and that it can be brought to a halt and then ridden on. Its movements throughout all these manoeuvres must be rhythmic and smooth. This section actually represents a sort of gymnastic work-out in preparation for the rigours of the succeeding days. Only a horse that obeys its rider *immediately* can be safely ridden over the complicated cross-country course which is the core of the three-day event. Only a horse capable of correctly using the thrust and carrying capacity of its quarters will be able sufficiently to reduce the strain on the tendons and muscles of its forelegs to be able to cope with all the fast and powerful high-jumps, long-jumps and finally jump-offs demanded of it on the final day.

Next, on **day two** the horsemen and horses go into the country. There are four separate phases of the day's tests: (a) a road section, trotting and slow-cantering over roads and tracks for about 6–12 miles (10–20 km); (b) a steeplechase done at full speed, over about 1–2½ miles (2–4 km) with 8–12 fences; (c) another road section, this time about 6 miles (10 km) long; and (d) a cross-country stretch, done at the gallop over 20–30 obstacles and a distance of about 3–5 miles (5–8 km). All of these details vary from event to event.

On the first road section the well trained horse warms up. It then has to develop great speed in the steeplechase, but can take the opportunity of recovering again on the second road section – and a properly trained horse will take full advantage of this. A short obligatory pause is followed by a veterinary inspection to check for signs of exhaustion, lameness, injury and general fitness. Finally comes the most difficult part: a fast ride over the most complicated and varied countryside possible with high-jumps, wide-jumps, combinations, ascents, descents and water-jumps. The latter are particularly unpopular with the horses, as they can't tell how deep the water is. Conversely, they're extremely popular with the public, who long to see someone fall in.

The cross-country section calls for a variety of things. Courage, intelligence, decisiveness, power and skill in both partners are taken for granted. Total obedience on the part of the horse is needed, as is the ability to make rapid evaluations, since many of the obstacles can be tackled from a variety of different angles. Most important of all is long, thorough, and careful training – of both horse and rider. The obstacles are fixed and made as complicated as possible: they are designed to terrify the rider as he looks them over on foot beforehand, but to prove possible for a horse to clear. Many can only be crossed if approached with sufficient speed and momentum to involve both horse and rider in split-second decisions.

On **day three** the showjumping takes place in the arena. The course is some 750–1000 yards (700–900 m) long and has 10–12 obstacles. The horse must have recovered from its exertions of the day before and still have sufficient reserves of strength left to complete a fault-free round.

What is really required on the second of the three days is, in essence, the same as in a heavy day's hunting, so perhaps it's not surprising that the English do well at horse trials. For centuries they have been breeding suitable horses for the sport: crossbreeds with a lot of Thoroughbred blood that have been tried for their strength and soundness in the hunt, and that can be ridden by

The momentum on take-off is all-important if a little horse like this is to clear such a huge obstacle.

children, the elderly, men and women with equal enjoyment. In England the conditions are as perfect for eventing as if specially tailored.

The English have developed a number of easier trials derived directly from heavy three-day eventing. Most notable is the one-day event or trial, where a considerably shortened and less strenuous version of the three-day programme is ridden. It amounts to a hunting course with a little dressage combined, followed by a simple showjumping circuit. It provides an alternative way of testing horses, one against the other, which would otherwise crowd and jostle together in the hunting field like old friends. On such a practical level, eventing is not only fun but beneficial both to horse and to rider.

Women are often world-leaders in the sport, and this is probably because of the hunting connection. In Great Britain, the Pony Club has been in existence since 1929 and currently has well over 50,000 members. Its main object is to train young people, up to the age of 18, to take their place in the hunting field, and so youngsters take part in a series of competitions designed with this end in mind.

Haute École

In the era in which the cavalry were still an effective war force, their horses had to be extremely agile and in close understanding with their riders. The life of the cavalryman quite literally depended on the ability of his horse to collect itself properly, turn in its own length, stop suddenly, move off quickly again, and so on. To achieve all these objectives it had not only to be ridden by a well trained horseman but to be extremely well schooled itself. These military horsemen and their mounts were magnificent.

During the sixteenth century the nobility took up the skills of the cavalry horse and turned them from a means of survival into an art-form; and in so doing they developed in Western Europe a type of riding quite different from anything else in the world. The Age of Mannerism had arrived

Below, *Robert Dover at the 1984 Olympics, where US riders won team and individual golds at showjumping and eventing.*

Right, *Patrick le Rolland of France performs a beautiful traverse to the left: just look at the crossed legs.*

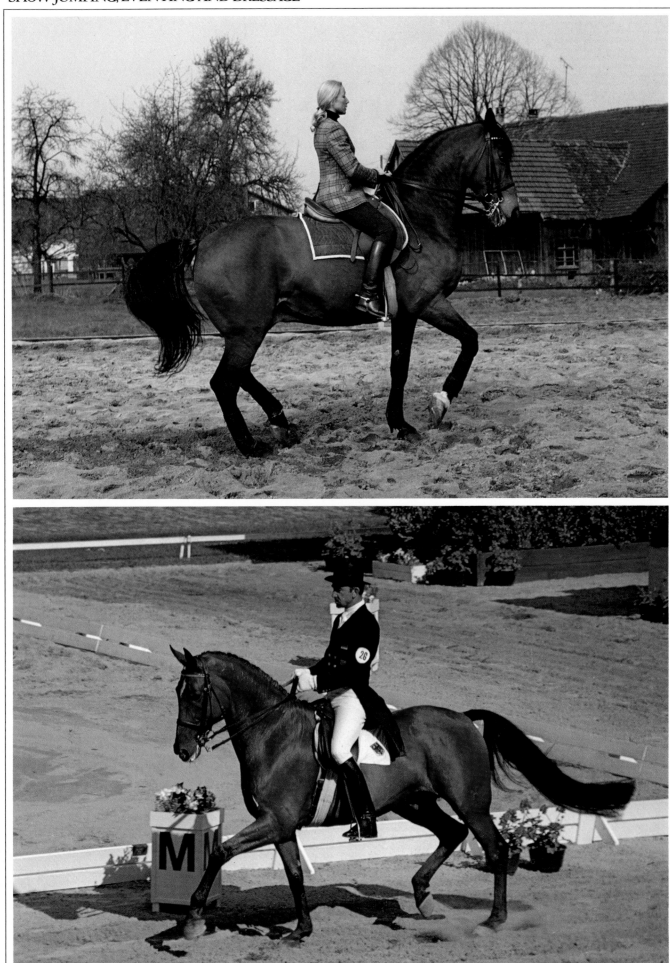

in the aesthetic world, and it was reflected in the lives of the aristocracy (at that time of history, nobody else really mattered, anyway). The ruling classes abhorred rough nature and turned to mannered and artificial activities, searching for virtuosity in all of life's arenas; in short, they became over-refined. Princelings saw themselves as brilliant personalities and their power as all-embracing. In Spain, France and Austria courtly life centred on magnificent new castles where almost all the aristocracy spent most of their time. Finding themselves in such close proximity with each other and with their ruler, they competed in many different ways to improve their social status and gain distinction in the eyes of their fellows.

Riding in the recently introduced *manège* – an open or covered riding area with a platform for spectators – was particularly well suited to this form of showing off, and so an important new role was created for the horse. For thousands of years it had been a helpmeet and a tool for mankind: now it was to be a highly stylized triumphal pedestal for riders who sought above all else to be *admired*. The needs of the horse were irrelevant; the effects it could produce were all.

In 1550 Federico Grisone published his *Gli Ordini di Cavalcare*, which is generally regarded as the first riding manual of modern times. It reflected the spirit of the epoch, which was to take a scientific approach to nature, to discover its laws and then make use of them. The horse was subjected to scientific scrutiny insofar as it could be within a limited training area – going out and observing a herd of wild horses didn't occur to anyone. The Academy at Naples was founded (and headed by Cesare Fiaschi, who taught Grisone), and the aristocracy of Europe flocked to it. In addition to the training in riding given in its covered *manèges* there were courses in dancing and swordsmanship: all three were highly relevant to the lifestyles of the new courtiers. The procedure used, whatever the discipline, was first to master the basic rules and then to move on in stages to a level of accomplishment that bordered on virtuosity. So the horseman learned the three gaits of walk, trot and canter within the limited space of the riding track, and then to shorten each gait more and more; and he was shown how to make the horse move sideways or turn itself around with the lightness and grace of a ballerina. The instructors at the Academy devoted themselves entirely to the refinement of this style of

riding; their fees could be afforded only by the richest or most favoured of courtiers. The most expensive horses were brought from far and wide.

In 1580 Archduke Charles of Austria founded a stud-farm at Lipizza using stallions drawn from Andalusia, Granada, Seville and from Polesina in Italy. From this stud-farm in due course came the Lipizzaner, a new breed especially developed for exhibition riding.

The various movements involved all had martial connotations, representing defensive and aggressive tactics. It is important to realize that in fact none of the movements required from the horse in either high-school work or dressage are unnatural: one has only to watch a crowd of lively young horses in a field for a while to see, sooner or later, every one of these movements executed spontaneously. The trot was developed in one direction into the sublime accentuated *Passage*, with its high bended knee; and in the other direction it was reduced to the *Piaffe*, the cadenced trot on the spot. The horses learned to rise up under their riders into the position known as the *Levade*, in which both forelegs were lifted off the ground so that the weight of the horseman was carried by the animal's rear legs. This is the position in which, traditionally, mounted kings and military heroes have been painted: Xenophon mentioned the fact, and the practice still continues today.

But even these movements were not enough for the mannered princes of the sixteenth century. In the *Courvette* (known also as the *Courbette*) the horse hops forward in the *Levade* position several times without allowing its forefeet to touch the ground. In the *Ballotade* it springs into the air with its legs drawn together. Finally, there is the *Capriole*, which represents the high-point of the 'airs above the ground': the horse jumps straight up into the air and kicks out vigorously with its hind-legs before landing again on the original spot.

The Lipizzaners have preserved the riding styles of that period right up until our own time. At the Spanish Riding School of Vienna, which was founded by the Austrian Imperial Court, they still today display 'schooling on and above the ground' to a fascinated public. A second centre which has preserved this classical style of riding is the 'Cadre Noir' of the French State Riding Institute at Saumur, although it cannot be described as sharing the magnificence of the Spanish Riding School.

Dressage
Modern dressage, as seen in tournaments and at international competitions, no longer recognizes the arts of the Haute École. It has become a much simpler and more practical affair, thanks to a long

Above left, Christine Stuckelberger from Switzerland practises the Piaffe – trotting on the spot.

Above right, Reiner Klimke of Germany, one of the world's foremost exponents of dressage, rides to perfection.

period during which it was dominated by military influences. The soldier had to transform a horse fresh from the pasture – a horse that was unaccustomed to carrying a load and saw no reason to be obedient to anyone – into a creature suitable for use in war, prepared to carry heavy loads, and ready to obey all commands instantly. The soldier therefore needed standard rules, and these were borrowed from the court riding schools. Military riding theorists worked on these rules for hundreds of years, modifying and adapting them better to suit the cavalry's purpose. As a result, diverse concepts and styles emerged – because in different countries horse and human had basically different relationships with each other. The horses differed in temperament, build and aptitude, and one could say almost exactly the same about their riders.

Left, *one of the most famous riders of all, Virginia Holgate on Priceless at the Badminton Trials in 1985.*

Below, *an Andalusian shows unmistakable presence as he performs the fast trot, or* Passage *with high bended knee.*

The area in which dressage activities take place is defined precisely: it is either 20 × 40 m or 20 × 60 m (21·8 × 43·7 or 21·8 × 65·6 yards). At the sides are fixed points at set distances from each other; during the lesson, all movements must be performed in exact relation to the relevant points. Horse and rider must imagine themselves to be held within a web, the threads of which are made up of straight lines and arcs, waves and circles, all of which must be ridden along with mathematical precision. And all the time the movements themselves become more and more difficult!

The purpose of all this is primarily to develop the muscles of the young horse by means of a definite programme of daily training: the horse must be brought to the state where it can use its newly acquired sense of balance to carry its rider without any difficulty. Upon this foundation the rest is built. The horse learns to transfer its own weight and that of its rider to its hindlegs, and then step forward in a lively manner with the weight still on those underset hindlegs. It is taught the three gaits of walk, trot and canter at both slow and fast speeds; and, on the command of the rider, how to vary the speed in a smooth,

This Piber-born Lipizzaner, Primo Siglavy Primavera from the Circus Knie, demonstrates two High School movements: (left) the Ballotade *and (right) the most difficult of all the High School movements, the* Capriole.

unbroken manner. It learns to shorten its pace so that the forelegs rise up with increasing dignity and the hindlegs become progressively more deeply underset. The high-point of this part of the training is the *Piaffe* (see page 123), where the horse trots on the spot: it rhythmically raises and lowers its legs in diagonally opposed pairs. After long and patient training, the muscles of the horse so develop that it can perform this difficult action – the legs are slanted almost underneath its body – with increasing grace and charm, its movements becoming smooth and apparently effortless.

Years of training are also required for the horse to learn how to move at the canter while changing from left- to right-handed leads within progressively shorter distances. The horse must learn to walk so that its hindfeet do not follow in the track of its forefeet but make a second set of tracks. It learns to turn on either its fore- or its hindlegs; to move in a precisely straight line even though its body is set at an angle to that line; and how to develop a pirouette from a standing canter by turning about itself on its inner hindleg while taking several cantering strides. Finally, it discovers how to glide diagonally from one side of the

track to the other in a sideways movement, with the outer legs crossing over the inner ones: when horses do this, they really do seem to be dancing like ballerinas.

The great sixteenth-century French riding master Antoine de Pluvinel once said: 'We should never smother the natural grace of the horse. Like the pollen of fruit blossom, it never returns once it has been wafted away.' If one can retain the natural, inbuilt charm of a large dressage horse, then to watch it sweep and glide along, showing full vibrant mastery of what it has been taught, is a bewitching experience. It can certainly be compared in aesthetic terms with the virtuoso performance of any other type of art.

Pure art, though, is no longer what international dressage is really all about: the Olympic dressage competition, which is the most famous, is about winning medals. In the early days of Olympic equestrianism, when the riders were all army officers mounted on the finest horses the State could buy, the French, Dutch and Danes dominated the medals table, taking turns in capturing the gold. Nowadays the sport is largely sustained by wealthy private individuals and by commercial sponsorship, although this, too, limits the number of nations that are likely to be successful. Since 1964, the individual and team golds have been won by either West Germany or Switzerland, with only two exceptions: the Soviet rider I. Kizimov took the individual gold in 1968,

126

and at the next Games, in 1972, the USSR won the team event. Even in 1980, when most of the world was at Moscow (where Elisabeth Theurer of Austria won the gold), at the 'substitute' Olympics at Goodwood the team gold was won by West Germany and the individual gold by Christine Stuckelberger of Switzerland.

Dressage is a sport which centres on elegance. The horses have to move elegantly, so that all of their figures, however difficult, must be performed as if they came as naturally as breathing. The dress of the riders contributes to this elegance, too: black boots, white breeches, black riding-coat (or tails), top hat, white gloves and the white tie or cravat (sometimes known as the stock). Even the facial expressions of the riders are likely to be important when it comes to the judges making an assessment of their performance! Elegance is all, not just in the Olympic arena but even in a dressage contest among the children at the local riding school.

In German-speaking countries such contests among the children are much more common than in the rest of the world, because there dressage is infinitely more than just a sport: it is a training system that runs right through riding at every level. The end result is that the style of riding in those countries is rather different from that seen in either Britain or the United States. It demands the highest concentration on the part of both horse and rider together with, from the instruc-

tor, a training that lasts a lifetime, instinctive 'feel', and a generous measure of empathy and understanding. A prerequisite for all three is, of course, talent. Either as a training system or as a sport, dressage makes very great demands.

Because of the different styles of riding shown by the various countries, it is very easy for the people from one country to say that the style of another country is somehow 'wrong' – for the Germans to say that a Briton's more relaxed control of the horse, allowing the animal to use its own initiative a lot, is really just sloppiness; and for an American to say that German horses and riders are overtrained and their riding style unnatural to the point of hilarity. But there is no single road to successful riding: all of them have their merits and their faults. The Mongols conquered most of the known world thanks to their horsemanship, yet they never went in for anything like dressage; but the old cavalry horses, trained to the highest degree, could win or lose wars, too – in the seventeenth century Rupert of the Rhine showed how to do both, and often in the same battle.

To say that dressage is in some way either inferior or superior to other forms of riding is, therefore, to miss the point. To be involved in the theory and practice of classic dressage is a fascinating, elegant and historically significant way of learning about and participating in the wonderful sport of riding.

HORSEBACK SPECTACULARS

Work, play and sport are interrelated in such a complicated way that it is frequently difficult to draw a clear distinction between them. Play often represents people's everyday work – but done by someone else in their leisure time. When play is regulated and controlled it becomes sport, and when sport is performed in front of an audience it can take on all the trappings of spectacle.

Wherever they take place, horseback spectaculars have their similarities. The motive of the participants is only rarely profit: usually it is glory, although in some cases, for example in Japan, it is individual spiritual advancement. Often the 'games' originally had some religious connotation, but over the centuries this has been forgotten, so that the spectacle has become ancillary to a secular festival of some kind, or has even become the core of the festival itself. The participants come along for the fun and for the thrill of achievement, and the spectators likewise are looking for excitement, for the exhilaration of vicariously flirting with danger. In the colourful turmoil of the horseback spectacular both participant and spectator can forget for a while the troubles and cares of everyday life.

Military Spectaculars

As has been described in earlier chapters, many sports had their origins in preparations for war. In Roman times the soldiers would hammer a man-sized stake into the ground in the middle of a broad track through their camp. Riders would gallop at it and hit out at it with their weapons as if it were an enemy; the worse the damage they did to it, the more points they scored. Not only was it good practice for when those soldiers were riding against a real enemy, it was soon found by the military to be good psychological training, too: the riders would fantasize about the 'enemies' they were hacking to pieces, and this would increase their ferocity in the real event. Riding against the *palus*, as the stake was called, continued right through the Middle Ages, proving to be especially useful in the training of

people whose occupations were normally far from warlike: the farmer could enjoy the game just as a game, without necessarily realizing that he was receiving military training. In much the same sort of a way, some American-football players received distinction in the Korean and Vietnam wars because of their ability to throw grenades with pinpoint accuracy.

In the course of time, the stake was replaced by the dummy figure of a human being, dressed in the costume of the enemy of the day – a Moor or a Turk, perhaps, armed with a shield and a sword and attached by a swivel arrangement to a heavy base. The attacker had to aim for the centre of the shield, and if his aim was off-target the dummy would spin around and swat his retreating back with its wooden sword.

Haute École was directly linked to the training exercises performed by the cavalry, and the connection was underlined when the movements were interspersed with exercises which involved attacking dummy figures. In one such Carousel in 1662, Louis XIV, *Le Roi Soleil*, dressed in the attire of a Roman emperor and before an audience of 15,000, hit 16 wooden Turks' heads 'with a grace that captivated the whole world', as one eye-witness put it.

In India officers of the British cavalry regiments used to test their expertise with sword and lance by uprooting each other's tentpegs in camp. Since this tended to lead to fights, the game was soon formalized, so that it became a question of trying to pick up a collection of tentpegs from the ground. The Hindus called this and other horse-back games *gend-khana*, and we still use the word 'gymkhanas' to describe festivals of mounted

---

Right, *a young Fulani horseman from Cameroon shows off a little on his fiery black stallion.*

Overleaf, Sechseläuten: *'Bedouins' of the* Züm Kämbel *guild in Zurich gallop around the fire which will drive out winter to make way for the approaching spring.*

games and exercises. African 'fantasias', described elsewhere, are likewise games that have their origins in practice for warfare.

However, you should not get the impression that *all* mounted spectaculars have to do with the military. Some, like the rodeo, are practice for work – or, at least, reflections of a work tradition. And some have their origins in ancient superstitions and beliefs.

The Zurich Sechseläuten is one of these and takes place in the spring, a time of celebration in many of the world's religions. In the Sechseläuten, winter is driven away – quite literally. An effigy of it is planted on a wooden post and hunted to the death, ending its life in the avid flames of a great pyre around which the horsemen gallop exultantly. Although early Christians dismissed it all as 'heathen idolatry', the festival survived until 1336 when it gained civic recognition and thereby a guarantee of further survival until at least the present day. The guilds were the ones who institutionalized it then, and in fact it is they who organize it still. In the Middle Ages, during the winter when the days were short, work would stop at five in the afternoon; but at the vernal equinox, when the days and the nights

A Hungarian csikós *(cowboy) rides the 'Hungarian Post'.*

were once more of equal length, would come a day when the bells of the Great Minster would ring instead at six o'clock to indicate the end of the working day (*Sechseläuten* = 'six bells'). Here was a signal that spring had at last arrived.

Today the Sechseläuten is still celebrated around the time of the equinox. There are colourful processions in historical dress, the centrepiece of which is the 'Böögg', a name related to our words 'bogey' and 'bogle'. At the end of the festivities the Böögg is put on a huge bonfire, just as in the days of old, and all the church-bells ring. As this awful snowman figure of winter goes up in flames, and the fireworks with which it has been stuffed fill the air with their explosions, the guildsmen of today – the spiritual if not the actual descendants of the medieval guildsmen who were responsible for ensuring the festival's preservation – ride round and round it to the cheers of the spectators.

Cowboy Spectaculars – the Rodeo
Nowadays, when we use the word 'cowboys' we tend to think only of the cattle-herders of North America, but of course they are to be found in many parts of the world: the gauchos of South America, the *csikóse* of Hungary, and the mounted herdsmen of many other countries, including for example the French Camargue. It is

The 'Hungarian Post' again, but with five horses. Bela Lenard, the horseman, wears Hortobagy-Puszta ceremonial costume.

difficult for us now to realize quite how lonely an occupation cattle-driving used to be, when there were no radios or fast motor-vehicles to keep the men in touch with the outside world. For perhaps months on end the cowboys would have no company except each other and their horses; naturally enough, when groups of herdsmen came together they sought any excuse to show off the skills in horsemanship and cattle-management they had acquired over the lonely years.

Each year in the Camargue, the region of the Rhône delta in the south of France, there is a festival called the Ferrade to celebrate the branding of the year-old calves. The yearlings are cut off from the rest of the herd by skilled cowboys and then driven in a wild pursuit as close as possible to the fire where the branding-iron is being heated to its menacing redness (the name 'Ferrade' comes from *le fer* = 'iron'). The steers are then seized by their horns and thrown to the ground by a twist of the neck.

In the stark openness of the steppes (*puszta*) of Hungary's Hortobagy plain, east of the River Tisza, are the mounted cowpunchers called the *csikóse*. Like their counterparts in North America, horses and riders have to endure long hours of enforced idleness interspersed with brief bouts of frenzied activity as they bring runaway steers back into the herd. Horses and riders have such a close partnership that the *csikós* hardly needs to give instructions at all. The same bond of trust and mutual understanding is shown in the games the *csikóse* play to while away the times of idleness, when nothing much is happening with the herd. Some of these displays can be incredibly acrobatic on the part of both mount and rider. The horses rear or double up as if they were made of rubber; or they lie outstretched on the ground while the cowboy stands on them wielding his *karikás*. This is a long whip – 30 feet (10 m) or more in length – made of braided leather, with a 20-inch (50 cm) handle decorated with inlays. The *csikóse* are virtuosos in their performances with these whips: the sound of the cracks carries a long way across the still steppes at night, telling the darkness of the cowboy's atavistic sense of jubilation. The different sounds the cowboys can make with their whips form a language whereby they can communicate with their horses.

More complicated games played among the

csikóse are reserved for festivals or holidays. A speciality is the 'Hungarian Post', where a *csikós* will stand with one foot on the rump of each of two horses, balancing himself by flexing his knees as the horses trot or gallop along in perfect synchronization. In a more advanced version five horses are used, the cowboy standing on a rear pair which follow three horses running abreast.

Some cowboy games turn up all over the world, for the obvious reason that they reflect tasks which must be performed by any herdsman, no matter where he might live. One such is calf-roping, usually associated in our minds with North America, and especially with the rodeo. Rodeos sprang out of impromptu demonstrations of bravado that took place when the cowboys had time off, money to spend, and as like as not too much to drink. Gathered in the saloons of the old Wild West, cowboys would talk about their life with the herds – and, as time wore on, boasts would be topped by more boasts until eventually money would be slapped down on the tables and a horse and a steer would be fetched so that the cowboys could prove their outrageous claims. The bet won or lost, the cowboys would settle back to drinking or, all too often, indulge in another of their favourite sports: fighting.

The first known formal rodeo took place in 1885. Nowadays there is an organization to govern the sport, the Rodeo Cowboys' Association, based in Denver, Colorado, which has nearly 4000 members and holds about 500 different events each year. There are a few professional rodeo riders who make their living out of these events, but most are amateurs – horse-breeders, farmers, cowboys and just plain enthusiasts of the sport. All of them are tough and supremely fit, and need to be. Paradoxically, the fewest accidents occur in bareback riding; there are more when the cowboys attempt to 'bust' a bronco with a saddle on; and most of all in the highly dangerous activity of riding the brahma bulls. Steer-wrestling and calf-roping bring their crop of broken bones and pulled muscles; but, all in all, serious accidents are very rare.

Full-scale rodeo-riding is found only in the western United States, Canada and Mexico. The riders are loners. There are no state or national teams, no trainers or special doctors, no government subsidies or any of the other supports that sportsmen in other fields have come to expect. The motivations of the rodeo-rider are two: money and, possibly more importantly, glory.

As this series of pictures shows, a great deal of skill is needed first to rope and then to bring down the steer at the rodeo. The sport is thrilling and immensely popular with the spectators, but it is also dangerous for the competitors.

Every cowboy is an experienced calf-roper: it is, after all, part of his job. But it's all rather different when it's done in the rodeo-ring rather than out on the pastures. At a given signal, a young steer is released into the ring and dashes frenziedly across it. As it reaches a certain point a cowboy on his horse will erupt from another part of the ring. The horses are trained to react at the moment the steer reaches the right place, and use their powerful quarters to shoot forward like an arrow from a bow. The job of the horse is now to get into such a position that its rider, lasso at the ready, is brought directly behind the calf. It has to judge the calf's movements exactly as it weaves around the arena, adjusting its own position without any instructions from the rider, until it has brought him into perfect position – a position it must now hold as the calf zigzags around on its unpredictable course. This leaves the cowboy free to concentrate on throwing his lasso.

After the calf is caught, the horse must keep the line taut – just as in real life out on the pastures – while the rider must leap from the saddle and run and tie the calf's legs with another rope. He must then undo the end of the lasso from the horse's pommel and both must wait for the calf to lie, unable to move, for a full five seconds before the calf-roping can be counted as complete. The winner of the contest is the one who does all this in the shortest time.

Obviously the horse is the cowboy's equal partner in calf-roping, whether it is being done at the rodeo or out on the ranch. The training required is extensive, and the cowboy must show considerable patience during it: the most important element is the daily work done with the herd. The big difference between the real situation and the rodeo is the time aspect: on the ranch it usually doesn't matter much how long the whole exercise takes, but in the rodeo-ring it is vital. If the horse accidentally runs past the steer or misjudges the distance between itself and the steer, vital seconds tick away; if the horse pulls up too slowly after the lasso has been thrown, the cowboy has to rush towards the steer from a standing start, losing further precious seconds. Conversely, if the horse pulls up too abruptly the cowboy can be thrown flat on his face. All sorts of other minor flaws in the horse's performance can mean the difference between winning and losing. Naturally, the horse can't do it all: the rider has to train himself, too. In particular, he must practise throwing his lasso with complete accuracy and control, and so rodeo-riders have the irritating habit of tossing their lassos at any convenient target: chickens, dogs, stools, fence-posts . . . Their friends and families learn to move around cautiously in case they suddenly find themselves being used for practice!

An exciting and more dangerous variant of calf-roping is steer-wrestling, which involves the cowboy grabbing a very fast young 700-pound (320 kg) steer by the horns and throwing it to the ground in a prescribed manner – taking only a few seconds to do so. Again the steer is released from a starting box into the arena, but this time it is flanked on either side by riders. The cowboy on one side has the job of keeping the steer running in a straight line, but it is his colleague on the other who has the real work to do. When he thinks the time is ripe, he must lean at an angle of 45° out of his saddle to grab the steer's horns. His horse must then outpace the steer, so that when the cowboy finally throws himself from the saddle his legs are pointing out towards the front; as he lands, he jams his feet into the sand in front of the steer's head, using his body as a brake to stop its progress.

The secret of throwing the steer down is to get it off balance, twisting it onto the ground before it has had a chance to recover. To do this the man himself must have excellent balance, and be able to use the weight and forward momentum of the steer to his own advantage. The cowboy must try to turn the steer's head towards him, and then heave with his shoulder against the steer to throw it to the ground. This can't be done just any old how: there are precise rules governing the performance, and every mistake costs points. Animals are unpredictable: the steer itself can make a total shambles of the whole affair by suddenly standing stock-still or by getting its legs in the way of the horse's. Still, the superlative masters of the sport can within a mere four seconds catch their steer, throw it to the ground and keep it there, lying on its side with all four legs stretched out.

The most famous feature of the rodeo, certainly in terms of public awareness outside the Americas, is the bucking contest. As everyone knows, the object is for a cowboy to stay astride a fiercely bucking animal. Three types of 'ride' are involved: a barebacked horse, a saddled horse, and a brahma bull. Most riders would quail at the thought of trying to ride a wild horse or a vicious wild bull – and so, indeed, did the early cowboys, which is why in the old days the challenge tended to be associated with large sums of money. Back in those days, when life was beginning to settle down although the Wild West was still quite

Left, *steer-wrestling calls for good teamwork, split-second timing, almost superhuman courage, and sheer brute strength. The horses play a vital role in this performance.*

Right, *believe it or not, some of the competitors in the bronc-riding contests actually enjoy themselves!*

genuinely wild, not only were the cattle on the enormous ranches still basically untamed but so were the horses: they were bought from the Indians or found among the herds that coexisted out on the prairies with the cattle. At some point they had to be broken in for working and this had to be done quickly, because the ranchers couldn't spare the personnel for the long, patient ways of gradual training. Men who were confident of their bronco-busting abilities, who had lavish supplies of either courage or stupidity – and, especially, who needed the money – would travel around as specialist horse-breakers. Taking their saddles as the sole tools of their trade, they would hire themselves out wherever a group of young, wild horses had to be 'busted'. They were prepared to sit on anything with four legs and show it who was boss. They had to be every bit as tough as the horses they were breaking; and soon they got into the habit of competing with each other to see who was the foolhardiest of all. The sport of bronco-riding (or bronc-riding) came into being, and is now an essential feature of any rodeo.

Precise rules are laid down for the rodeo event. In saddle bronc-riding a modified stock saddle is used, smaller than the standard Western saddle and without a horn (pommel), while the rein is merely a rope attached to the horse's halter. A 'bucking strap' is tightened around the animal's flank to encourage its action. Horses and the going order are both drawn by lot. Before the ride begins, the cowboy lowers himself into the starting chute and onto the back of the horse he has drawn. When he has securely wrapped the rope around one hand, he signals for the gate to be opened, at which point the horse bucks wildly out into the ring. The rider is required to place his spurs on the horse's shoulders at the start and to use them on the first jump out of the chute. The actual ride, which must last 10 seconds, calls for fine balance and timing to gain maximum scores.

Scoring for bronc-riding follows a recognized procedure. Two judges each award from 0 to 25 points for the rider's performance, and the same range of points for the horse's – hence the reason that the cowboys hope to draw difficult mounts. The aggregate of the two scores is the rider's tally for that round. The rider can be disqualified for changing his hands on the rein, for touching the horse with his free hand, or, of course, for being thrown before the 10 seconds is up.

Bareback bronc-riding requires both skill and a good deal of brute strength. The rider is allowed to use only one hand to hold the grip, which is attached to a strap around the horse's girth. Rules and scoring are the same as in saddle bronc-riding, except that the ride has to last 8 rather than 10 seconds. Once again, the rider's free hand

should wave in the air to show that it is not touching the horse or assisting the other hand on the grip. There is no protective headgear.

People often ask if bronc-riding is not rather cruel, to which the obvious response is that, yes, it is: to the riders. The horses have to buck for a maximum of 8 or 10 seconds (less if they throw their rider) twice in any week; then they have a week's holiday before their next foray into the ring. The only horses to be used are those which have failed to respond to normal saddle-training, and this regulation is one reason why bronc-riding is becoming rarer. Thanks to systematic breeding over the generations, it is hard to find enough horses which haven't had all the necessary wildness bred out of them. Even then, the broncos are often quite docile before and after their brief encounter with the cowboy: they've learnt that the more they buck, the more likely that the unwelcome load will be removed from their backs, and afterwards they usually trot off quite happily, having, as it were, proved their point and shown who really *is* boss.

The horses are never injured in the contests, but the riders sometimes are. As described earlier, there are more accidents in saddle bronc-riding than in the bareback version: this is because of the stirrups which, while they certainly give the rider a more secure seat on his mount, can all too easily cause hazards, should he fall, by tangling up his feet, so that he may be dragged around the ring by a far from friendly horse. That said, the increasingly popular custom of fitting a small electrical gadget in the haunch-strap to 'ginger up' any horse that seems to need it should be discontinued – even though, in 8 or 10 seconds, it does only a fraction of the harm to the horse that some savage training methods used in other equestrian sports can do. No action that causes distress to the animal can be condoned in any game purporting to be sport: it is the thin end of the wedge, and inevitably leads to gross abuse.

Brahma-bull riding is particularly dangerous, since a bull will chase and gore an unseated cowboy. Riders are permitted to use both hands on the girth-grip; as with bareback bronc-riding, they have to try to stay on until the sounding of an eight-second buzzer.

Another standard rodeo event is reserved for women: barrel-racing. Three oil drums are set up in a large triangle, and the object is to ride round them in a sort of cloverleaf pattern. The horses start in a tight clockwise circle around the first drum; then cross to the second drum which they

Above, *the hat has gone but not the rider . . .*
but (below)
the bronc always wins in the end.

Above, *the saddleless events present an even greater challenge to the courage and skill of the competitors.*

Right, *women at the rodeo take part in the barrel-racing event. Here a contestant rounds the barrel and makes for home.*

must circle in an anticlockwise direction; then on to the third drum which they must go around clockwise; then finally at full gallop back to the starting line. The winner is the rider to complete this fastest, the whole course taking no more than a few seconds.

Rodeos are colourful affairs, and of course they are thrilling, too – that's the whole point of them. But the great feature that must appeal to the horse-lover is that at no stage are the horses required to do anything but things that come naturally to them or which they have been gently and patiently trained to do. The ones who are taking the risks are the cowboys and cowgirls, not the horses.

An African Fantasia

A desert town in Chad. There is not a breath of air, and the temperature is 45°C (113°F) in the shade – which wouldn't be so bad, except that the 'shade' is only a narrow strip of shadow along the base of a sun-baked wall. The streets are scorched brown; the dust is dark beneath the hooves of small horses that you can barely see because of the ornate silverwork and the saddlecloths and skins with which they are covered. The riders, dressed from head to foot in ceremonial garb,

their heads close-shaven, their scarves fluttering loosely in the wind of their motion, draw their swords as they gallop at full speed. In a great cloud of dust, they pull up before a sultan, sitting his horse majestically under a baldachin and surrounded by his retinue, and salute him. Troop by troop, the riders race up the long straight course to pull up their mounts only a few feet from their ruler. They are warriors on horseback.

You are witnessing a mounted spectacular in Africa. In this case the occasion is the visit of the sultan; another time it might be a great gathering of the clans, as tribes from widely scattered parts of the country come together to trade, to celebrate, and to discuss plans – not to mention showing off to each other.

We can use the word 'fantasias' to describe these displays, because that is really what they are. They represent dream-memories of times when the Holy Wars were in progress, or when no tribe was safe from a sudden, unheralded attack from its neighbour. The riders are acting out their ferocious response to aggression: counter-aggression, the lightning attack. Nowadays, as for the last few centuries, the peoples of North Africa and the Near East use their camels for daily transport, reserving their horses for fantasias – in the same way that the horses were once reserved for use in repelling unexpected attacks. Today those attacks, if they occur, involve armoured vehicles, rifles and rockets, but the tradition lives on. In the fantasia the weapons are there only for symbolic purposes and to allow the riders to demonstrate skill in their use, either as individuals or as a group.

Fantasias are found all around the Sahara, in Chad, Cameroon and Morocco, and almost always with local royalty as their centrepiece. Whatever the country, the fantasias share various things in common: the squads of riders in their flamboyantly colourful costumes, the crowds of excited spectators, the spirit of self-glorification among the participants, and their almost paradoxical demonstration of subservience to their rulers. The display takes place in a long rectangular space, with the aristocrats tented along one of the short sides and the public gathered along one of the long ones. Down this stretch race the troops of warriors at full gallop, their mounts straining with speed, to pull up at the last moment in front of the rulers. One moment they are moving in symbolic attack; the next they are acknowledging their loyalty.

Fantasias are always ridden with several abreast – how many depends upon the width of the space available – and the horses must be kept as close to each other as possible to form a solid wall of attacking menace. Sometimes this can be trans-

formed in an instant into the most astonishing gentleness. The author recalls once seeing three riders urged on to the wildest gallop by the crowds, 'attacking' a line of singing girls, their swords gleaming high in the bright sunshine. The girls didn't miss a note as the horses reared up inches away from them; and as the forehooves dropped back to the dust the riders leant forward and, with the utmost gentleness, tapped each girl on the shoulder with their naked, wickedly sharp swords. At other times, by contrast, it can all go wrong, as terrified horses plough into the crowds, their hooves lashing out to break ribs and arms and legs. The very real dangers of the event are a part of its excitement.

Just as in rodeo, the question of cruelty to the horses performing in these spectacles comes up. The horses are ridden with harsh bits, and driven forward by being kicked in the ribs with the side of the stirrup-shoe. They are launched like a bullet into the gallop, and pulled up in a cloud of dust, rearing and slithering along in the sand on their quarters. Only in the saddle can you judge whether or not there is any cruelty involved. Acclimatizing yourself to the strange stirrups, you hold the reins loosely in a couple of fingers and walk the horse to the start. At a sign from the starter you give the horse a press with the smooth side of the stirrup-shoes and – *thump!* – you are thrown back against the wooden edge of the saddle as the horse rockets into motion. Your lower legs are drawn up and back, and instinctively you push your knees sharply forward, into the movement, and *fly*. Balanced surely on top of your mount, the reins forgotten in your fingers, you are free to forget everything except the thrill of the short, frenzied gallop. Carried along willy-nilly into the orgasmic conclusion of the 'attack' (the *chok*), you find yourself crying '*Bii* . . . *Biii* . . .' just like all the others, instinctively tugging sharply on the reins as the sovereign's tent comes rapidly and menacingly closer, and then being thrown against the back of your saddle once again as the horse rears, slithering to a stop. It's all over.

The truth is that, after taking part in the fantasia, you are not really too sure about what actually happened – except that, as far as you can remember, the horse did all the work. You were, quite literally, only along for the ride. The horses are all too keen to race off at the start; and at the other end they know perfectly well exactly where they've got to stop. As in any other riding activity, the better the rider, the better the horse will perform, something which is especially im-

These African warriors approach their local leader at a full gallop, reining back just in time to come to a screaming halt in a cloud of dust.

143

Above, *the horse in the foreground, caught by a ray of evening sun, shines like shimmering silver.*

Below left, *the furnishings of the ceremonial tent lie waiting to be put in their allotted places.*

Below right, *the protective hand of Fatima is painted in a bold red on the chest of this very special mare.*

pressive when you consider that the only means the rider has of communicating with his mount is by word of mouth. These riders have natural talent. No one has ever told them that they should lift themselves up in the saddle to take the weight off the horse's back; they just do it. Nevertheless, the real credit must go to the horses: one could train a Quarter-horse for years

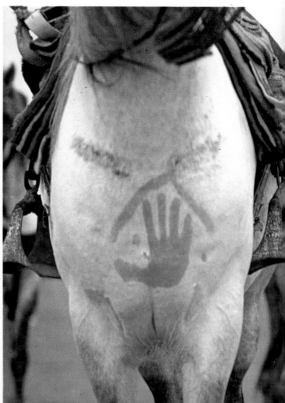

The fettered stallion swishes his tail before settling down to eat the meal which has just been delivered.

on end and it would still never be able to perform a sliding halt with the perfection and exactitude of these African mounts.

Bull-Fighting
The same cannot be said about bull-fighting, which on any level is a barbarous sport. The centrepiece of it is, of course, the torture and slaughter of the bull; ancillary to it is the very real danger of horses and men being gored to death or hideously maimed. However much people try to glamorize the sport, if such it can be called, the fact remains that it is a brutal and bloody business. In hunting one can say that the object is not really the rending to pieces of the luckless wild animal chosen as prey – the chase is the thing, it doesn't really matter if it is unsuccessful – and that anyway the pain is short and the victim an agricultural pest; but none of these defences are valid in the case of bull-fighting. To be sure there is a thrill as mounted or running men gamble with their lives; but the necessary heart of the spectacle is the tormented death of the bull.

For this and other reasons it would be tempting to omit all mention of bull-fighting from this book . . . but that would be to ignore the facts that it is

in many ways a horseback spectacular, and that the horses which take part are trained as patiently and thoroughly as they are for any other equestrian event. Still, we have no need to follow the procedure all the way into the arena: we can learn just as much about it by concentrating on its bloodless aspects.

A distant ancestor of modern bull-fighting was practised in the ancient Mediterranean region, and there still survive scenes painted on decorated vases showing the game in progress. In bull-dancing, as we can call it, teams of acrobats would perform daring antics on, over and in front of the bull, which not unnaturally became maddened by the frenzy of activity. At this remove in time, it is impossible for us to be certain what the main purpose of the game actually was: to dominate the bull, as in modern North American steer-wrestling (another bloodless form of bull-fighting), or simply to demonstrate the daring athleticism of the acrobats and their contempt both for danger and for the comparatively slug-

145

gish movements of the infuriated bull. As far as can be made out, though, the game was in effect an addition to the basic repertoire of all travelling acrobats and tumblers since history began, although more recent entertainers have had more sense! It seems likely that the ritual was practised for the amusement of rulers by trained slaves; in short, that the dangers didn't matter too much because what was the life of a slave, one way or another? At any event, it seems that the motives weren't connected with hurting or killing the bull: the animal was simply being used as a source of unpredictable hazard for the acrobats to demonstrate their courage and skills against. In a few parts of the world bull-fights can still be found where exactly the same motives are in operation, where the bull is the last thing to be hurt, where in fact it is a sign of failure on the part of the human participants if the bull twists a leg. But these places are sadly few and far between; it's blood the crowds want.

Since about the eighteenth century when the aristocracy picked up the idea from the Moors, Spain has been the spiritual home of bull-fighting. There, horses are involved in the arena to carry the picadors, whose job it is to stab at the muscles of the bull's neck so that its head drops, ready for the matador to show off his capework. In Portugal horses are involved in many more aspects of the bull-fight. Much more interesting from our point of view, however, is the role played by horses in the preparation and selection of the bulls for the arena. Each year, out on the great estates of the cattle-breeders, the year-old calves are taken in the spring and tested to see if they are wild and spirited enough to become future fighting bulls or if they should simply be put with the rest of the herd for fattening. These tests are carried out by mounted bull-fighters.

The rider must train his horse by exercising it very hard in a restricted space. He practises making his horse stand still, turn, gallop, and take tight bends at speed; both must get used to vaulting, with and without reins. Once rider and horse are able to work in perfect harmony, it is time to practise with the calves. Bending low out of the saddle, the rider will first of all entice the calf with a cap in his outstretched hand, and then goad it into aggressive response. The slightest of pressures on the reins will bring the horse to an abrupt halt; it needs no instruction from its rider to speed to safety as soon as the calf's horns come too close. These horses are superbly trained, intelligent and obedient.

The rider wears leather pads over his jeans, and his feet, clad in the characteristic short Andalusian boots, are put into the stirrups as far as the instep. In his right hand the rider holds his banderilla, a short barbed lance that is jabbed once – and once only – into the neck of each young cow during the trials. The only spectators are the rider's colleagues on the estate and, in the box, the stud-manager and the veterinary surgeon, both watching intently every movement of the calf.

Of course, this is not bull-fighting proper: it's only a test, and the calves don't get hurt . . . much. Still, it is difficult to draw one's attention away from the fight to concentrate instead on the rider and his mount. No picture can reproduce the suppleness of their movements together, the way they pirouette in front of the loudly bellowing calf, the way they almost dance in front of its snorting nose. The rider roars defiantly at the angry beast, hounding it with shouts and gestures, before pushing the horse away in a weaving traverse and then returning to execute a swift, graceful volte around the little cow. It is easy to fall under the spell of these horses which, with their calm riders, meet danger with a virtual serenity – the easy grace that comes from perfect body-control. It is just a pity that this splendid dance should be the precursor of such brutality in the bull-ring.

Yabusame

At the other side of the world – in every sense of that expression – from war-games and cowboy games is the Japanese mounted spectacular known as Yabusame. The motivation couldn't be more different. It is not mere sport or self-aggrandisement but spiritual enhancement: Yabusame is an important part of ancient religious ceremonies and is performed so that people may advance along the *tao* of self-realization.

Firing a bow from horseback at the enemy is an age-old fighting technique used by the horse-riding people of central Asia – the Mongols and the Turkomans, the Scythians, the Huns and the Magyars. All these peoples mastered the tactics of 'victory in flight': immediately after a first attack they would retreat like lightning and then, twisting around backwards in their saddles while they moved at full gallop, unleash wave after wave of arrows into their foes with terrifying accuracy. This is difficult enough for people growing up in cultures where horse and rider are throughout life in such close cooperation with each other that they become almost like centaurs. With the best will in the world, it cannot be said that the Japanese are a culture like that; they have no great tradition of riding in instinctive unity with their

The enthusiastic children crouch at the front of the brightly clad crowd eagerly watching the squads of fantasia riders as they make their spectacular obeisance to the sultan and lenidos in Chad. Drama and colour are the keynotes of the fantasia.

horses, and for obvious reasons their history is not littered with examples of great cavalry conquests. Yet, when Japanese mounted archers take part in Yabusame, it is difficult to think of any rider who sits his horse with more poise and grace: it is as if the archer had forgotten his own body and that of the horse and was being transported through the willing air, concentrating all his attentions on the enormous decorated bow, the arrow and the target.

The ceremony of Yabusame is said to have been introduced in 1096 by the Emperor Shirakawa. Over the centuries its popularity has often wavered, but never quite disappeared. In order to understand it, you have to realize that in Zen the act of archery has lost all its military connotations. According to one commentator, Daisetz Suzuki: 'In the performance, consciousness is to be harmoniously assimilated with the unconscious. Defence and attack are not polarized opposites; they are one complete reality. The archer must be quite relaxed and detached from himself to become one

Above, the Fulani, in Cameroon, arrives with all the members of his family to greet his king.

Right, a member of one of the rich cattle-breeding families rides on his majestic way to watch the bull-fight.

with the technical accomplishment of the act. Only if he forgets that he is firing, that there is an arrow and a target, will his arrow hit the target with unfailing accuracy.' Many people throughout the world who are involved in equestrian and other sports recount that sometimes, in the course of their sport, they too reach this strange state of complete immersion in what they are doing, so that they no longer have to *try* to perform perfectly: they just let it happen. However, to many Westerners the whole idea is completely alien; so perhaps all we can hope to do is see Yabusame as a sport – but what a graceful, thrilling sport it is.

The exercise always takes place close to a large

temple, and the 'master of ceremonies' is the high priest of that shrine. Beforehand all the participants kneel and take a sip of holy wine from a small goblet offered to them by the priests. Following a strict ritual, each rider correctly adjusts the folds of his garb and then puts his sword (or swords) into the scabbard; the arrows, the bow and the horse are then blessed. Now the riders are ready to move off in a ceremonial procession, led by the high priest on a white horse, to the Yabusame course. The course is about 240 yards (220 m) long and about 8 feet (2·5 m) wide; it is fenced off on both sides with posts and ropes. There are three square targets mounted on poles at intervals along the left-hand side of the course.

The participants are dressed in magnificent fifteenth-century samurai costumes. These are cherished family heirlooms, passed down from generation to generation; if a new one has ever to be made, the original design is copied in perfect detail. The horses used are native stallions. Each rider is equipped with a longbow – about 7 feet (2·15 m) long – and a quiver of arrows. He wears a light body-armour made of varnished wood over his heavy silk robes. The stallions, too, are flamboyantly decorated with silk bindings and fringes and woollen tassels. The horses' headgear is made of embroidered braid in a style which was already current by the sixth century: it has sidepieces and a bit – rectangular, oval or circular in cross-section – made of gilded bronze or iron. The saddle has a narrow seat made of lacquer and decorated leather; the rider's feet fit into *shitanagas*, small lacquered wooden clogs.

Suddenly everything goes quiet as the first competitor rides up to the start. His stallion is held by two assistants while he throws the reins over the pommel of the saddle. At the sound of a gong the stallion is let loose to shoot away like a bullet along the narrow strip of track, kicking up clumps of sand from its hooves, with its head and neck stretched as far forward as they will go. The

Below, *as he tests the calf for the bull-fight, the rider is protected by leather pads – but not so the horse.*

Right, *the arrow is released as this Yabusame archer, dressed in full Samurai costume, gallops at top speed past the target.*

archer must shoot at each of the three targets as it flashes by. To realize just how difficult this is, and how precisely the gallop of the horse must be paced, just imagine that you have to reach back over your shoulder three times during a brief gallop to draw an arrow, nock it onto the string, aim it, and release it at precisely the right moment as you zip past the target. Tiny fractions of a second separate perfect attainment from undignified ignominy, and yet all the time the archer is doing this he is careering along at full speed on top of half a ton of stallion!

Every rider completes five rounds, and the winner is awarded a white chrysanthemum.

Legend has it that the archers of the past were so good at concentrating their spirits and life-force that they could hit a fly in flight. This is probably hyperbole, but a modern master has claimed to have put a first shot right in the middle of the target when firing in total darkness, and then fired a second arrow which split the first right down the shaft. He was not, however, mounted at the time. The important feature of Yabusame is that the moving horse introduces the same degree of difficulty as for the master

firing in pitch darkness. Eyes and hands, bow and arrow, form an integral system controlled by breathing and meditation until they achieve a complete mix of harmonious consciousness – and the target is hit. In fact it *has to be* hit, because there is no other logical resolution of the system that has been set up by the rider's body and mind.

But merely hitting the target is not enough to satisfy the judges. The exercise must be accomplished with complete beauty of movement. The speed of the horse as it races down the track and the bearing of both horse and rider play a part in the judges' deliberations, and affect the final selection of the winner. But this is not the studied elegance of, say, a dressage contest. It is not something that can be trained for, in itself. The long courses of meditation and inner contem-

Below, *thanks to the Yabusame archer's frame of mind, it becomes almost inevitable that the arrow will hit the target.*

Right, *the rider is using his horse only as a vehicle: his attentions are concentrated on the archery.*

plation which the riders undergo do not have elegance as their goal. What happens is that the riders achieve a certain state of mental awareness and harmony, of which grace and elegance are inevitable by-products.

This state is occasionally attained, either accidentally or deliberately, by Western sportsmen in all disciplines and of all standards. It is quite unmistakable when it occurs. It is as if one can just stand back and watch while one's body scores the goal, guides the horse over the jump, or serves the untouchable ace right down the line.

In all games which are really tough for the riders, such as at the rodeo, the horse is rarely if ever taken to the limits of its ability and is certainly not placed under the stress which arises in more regimented sporting contests such as showjumping and eventing. In the sports discussed in this chapter the horse is usually a specialist, which through training has learned to apply its simple, natural abilities in such a way that it constantly improves them. Premature degener-

ation, therefore, rarely affects the horses involved in these games.

The same is true, if not even more so, of the horses which take part in Yabusame. They are required to go through a series of five short, fast gallops, which is exactly what their bodies are designed to do in the wild in order to flee from dangers. They are not affected in any way by the release of the arrow (and neither should the rider be), because the whole point of the exercise is that the arrow should be released effortlessly. During the gallop, the horse is not even under the control of reins and bit: it is running free.

This, indeed, is the common feature of all of the great horseback spectaculars. Not the crowds, not the thrills, not the contest between human beings and their physical limitations, but the fact that the role of the horses involves them in using nothing more than their natural abilities and mainly behaving as they would in the wild. This is the great beauty of all the games, the spectaculars, described in this chapter.

POLO

The name 'polo' is probably derived from the Tibetan word *pulu*, which means a root, from which the wooden ball used in the game can be made. Centuries ago a version of polo was being played on the steppes of central Asia; long before Christ the Chinese were already familiar with a mounted ball-game, which they had learned from the Mongols; and at about the same time the Medes and the Persians were also playing it. From Persia the game travelled into Asia Minor; and it was taken into India – where much later the English were to pick it up – by both the Chinese and the Mongols.

A famous tale of dubious authenticity concerns Alexander the Great and the game of polo. When Alexander succeeded his father, Philip II, to the throne of Macedon he pointedly informed Darius III, Emperor of Persia, that he didn't plan to continue paying him any tribute – and would resist with as much force as necessary any efforts at its collection. Darius' response was to send him a polo-stick and a ball, the clear implication being that Alexander was still a sprig of a youth and would be better off concentrating his attentions on youthful games, rather than on more grown-up activities such as war. Alexander offered profuse thanks for the gift, saying that he realized it was meant to be allegorical: the ball symbolized the Earth and the stick symbolized himself!

Polo was the first mounted game to have fixed rules and thus to be considered fair and safe enough for the aristocracy to take part: earlier mounted team games were much rougher and more impromptu. A record of the rules survives from third-century Persia; while in the fifth century the game was played by the Byzantine Emperor Theodosius II. He allowed the affairs of state to be run by two domineering women, his sister Pulcheria and his wife Eudocia, and concentrated instead on a life of diversion and pleasure. As part of this, he had a covered polo hall built in Constantinople so that he could play the game in all weathers.

For a long time horses and equipment were exported to most parts of the world from Turkestan, and the appeal of this fiery, strenuous and dangerous game spread rapidly. During the seventh and eighth centuries it travelled from India to Japan and back to China, from where it had come in the first place.

For millennia this type of equestrian competition was to be found only in Asia, but in the middle of the nineteenth century the English discovered it in India. In 1859 the oldest polo club in the world was founded by officers there – the Silchar Polo Club – and in 1871 the game was brought to England itself by a group of army officers. Very soon afterwards, in 1874, it was introduced to South Africa and two years later, in 1876, to the United States. Today England, Argentina and the United States head the polo-playing nations.

The game is played between two teams of four players each on an area 300 yards (274 m) long and 150 yards (137 m) or so wide. The exact dimensions of the pitch may vary. The two goals must be at least 250 yards (227 m) apart, and the aim is to get the ball into the enemy goal. The game is divided into a variable number of phases – four, six, seven, or eight – called 'chukkers', each of which lasts about 7½ minutes. The teams change ends after each chukker or whenever a goal has been scored. The ball is made of willow or bamboo root, and has a diameter of 3¼ inches (8 cm); it is hit using a polo-stick, called a mallet in the United States, which consists of a long stick of sycamore, bamboo or ash with a wrist-strap at one end and, at the other, a piece of wood set at right angles.

If one imagines a wooden ball hit with full force as a yardstick for speed, the demands placed on the horses' health, swiftness and agility can easily be imagined. For a full 7½ minutes, non-stop, the polo-pony must run, stop, spin around, perform sharp twisting bends at breakneck speed and

Polo is a fast and potentially dangerous game, requiring team spirit.

avoid all the other horses, while at the same time gluing its eyes to the ball, following it at top speed, and scarcely if ever having the slightest moment's pause for a quick breather. It's not surprising that after each chukker the ponies are changed, so that each rider requires at least three mounts for a single game. Each pony requires an individually tailored or selected outfit comprising a polo saddle, bridle and leg bandages or boots, while different polo-sticks must be used in accordance with the varying heights of the mounts ridden during the game. The ponies need to be trained for the sport and transported to matches, and, when they are not playing, still require stables and plenty of exercise as well as grooms to look after them. In short, a lot of money is needed; and for this reason the game was in the past confined to princes and, later, the military. Nowadays it is in most countries still the prerogative of only the very rich.

Originally polo-ponies were small and wiry, like all the native horses of Asia. They were limited in size to 13·3 hands by rules introduced by the English when they adopted the game. In 1890 this restriction was relaxed a little, allowing another ½ hand (5 cm) of height, and in 1901 the limit was pushed up still further, to 14·2 hands. In 1919 all size restrictions were abolished. These

Above, these Iranian polo ponies from Abadan are small and wiry, fast and manoeuvrable – ideal for polo.

Right, on the far side of the world, polo at Palm Beach. The venue may change, but the game is just as fast and furious.

progressive relaxations of height restrictions were attempts to increase the availability of suitable horses, and thereby to reduce the prices; in fact, with the introduction of Thoroughbreds to the sport, the price went up rather than down. Nowadays, 15 hands is generally considered an ideal height for a polo-pony. Among the reasons for this are that riders find the smaller horses infinitely more manoeuvrable and also that it is far easier to hit the ball from a small, fast-moving mount than from, say, a racehorse with its longer legs.

The indispensable prerequisites for a polo-pony were and still are speed, courage, stamina, a good sense of balance, a positive attitude towards games and a temperament that is neither too sluggish nor too excitable. Around 1930 the Argentinian polo-pony dominated the scene: of Thoroughbred stock, it had gained plenty of additional toughness on the country's cattle-farms and had a superior bone structure. Nowadays this 'pony', which has come to have a height of about 15·2 hands, makes a welcome contribution to Argentinian exports.

As with any equestrian sport, one must consider whether or not it is cruel to the horses. In many ways, when watching a game of polo, it has to be said that it *looks* as if it is. The ponies' wide-open mouths are an obvious feature, and they are also decorated with a lot of leather. Nearly all have a martingale, a strap leading from the girth up between the front legs to the noseband, designed to prevent them from throwing their heads up too high. This is quite important: if the horse was allowed to throw its head back at the same time that the rider was throwing *his* head forward to make a shot, a lot of teeth would be lost! Another noticeable point is that riders do not use the bit for control, but rely instead on neck reining – that is, they signal to the horse by use of the feel of the reins on either side of its neck.

On balance, then, one may conclude that polo is a game that is as much fun for the horses as it is for their riders – not to mention the spectators.

Overleaf, *polo is never a poor man's game, but in South Africa every farmer owns horses.*

RIDING FOR PLEASURE

Riding as a sport has been the subject of much of this book so far, but this chapter explores, through words and pictures, another equally valid form of mounted adventure: riding for pleasure. The two types of riding are of course different, and at advanced level have to be learned differently, but they share a single golden rule: the more relaxed someone is when riding, the more relaxed the horse will usually be. Conversely, it is easier to be relaxed on a horse which is content with its lot than on a highly strung animal which loathes the restrictions on its activities which people have enforced. It is possible that some sporting horses are better off kept in closed stables; but there is no question that the average horse for leisure-time riding is far more contented and more easily able to develop the best points of its character if it is allowed to roam in ample pastures with others of its own kind.

Horses are allowed to live in this free way in many countries today – most notably in North America. And one of the great joys of our technological age is that never before have so many people been able to travel abroad to see horses in their natural state. It has become possible, and in some cases actually easy, for horse-lovers to explore the world of the horse at first hand. Special trips are organized whereby you can travel halfway across the planet to visit a famous race or a gymkhana, or to take part in an international auction. We can see stud-farms, visit equestrian museums, or watch the Lipizzaner horses on display in Vienna. Closer to home, we can go to the races – or, much more exciting, find a vantage point from which to watch racehorses being exercised in the mists of the early morning. We can have an afternoon picnic on a hillside where horse trials are in progress and watch the horses and their riders skilfully manoeuvring their way through the cross-country course. On a cold winter's evening we can experience all the thrills of the climax of a trotting race – but protected by the glass of the stands from the chilly winds or the icy drizzle.

Almost without exception, throughout the Western world the horse is no longer a necessity: we don't need it to do work for us, to fuel our vanity, to get us from place to place, or to serve us as a status symbol. Our basic relationship with the horse has changed. For the first time in history, people can choose the horse they want rather than the horse they need: we don't have to have a heavy horse because there's work to be done on the land or heavy goods to be transported; we don't have to have a fast, nervous carriage-horse to draw us along the road in our coach; we don't need a great war-horse to carry us and our armour into battle; we don't even have to pick a smart, elegant horse for our leisure-time riding in order to keep up appearances. We can choose to ride whatever type of horse we happen to get along with – assuming, of course, that it is suitable and fit to ride. We can opt for a Shetland pony, a Thoroughbred, a good-natured Fjord horse, a comfortable Paso Fino from Peru, a Camargue horse, an English Cob, one of those tough, undemanding horses from Poland . . . the list is almost endless. The horse of our dreams can be large or small, fat or thin, swift or plodding, from a long and distinguished pedigree or a mixture of every strain known to mankind and a few others besides. And we can decide whether we want a horse just to be a peaceful companion for our leisure hours or to take part in all the exciting hurly-burly of equestrian sports.

Mounted Adventures

In a sense, every encounter with horses is an adventure, and more and more people are wanting to participate in such adventures.

What could be more enjoyable than the feel of sun, wind and water on bare skin as we gallop in the summer along the edge of the sea or through the shallows of a ford? What could bring greater

With quiet confidence this little girl rides a horse that is much more than just a pet: it's a household friend.

excitement to our senses than the close association with a powerful, muscular horse which shares in all our adventures? For horses *are* sensual creatures; they smell good, feel good, and can match the exuberance of our mood. They don't just carry us from place to place in a dull way, like an automobile; no, because of their own strength and their enjoyment of moving freely they make the going much more important than the getting there. And horses never let us forget that they are individuals with individual wills.

Although summer is the season most often associated with leisure riding, horses can be a part of your life all year round. Horses need exercise, and should be ridden in all weathers. People need to be taken out in all weathers, too! Soon you find that there is no such thing as *bad* weather any longer, just *different* weather – for which you have to dress differently. Fog and snow bring their own pleasurable sensations; early darkness is no longer a threat when riding

A family concern of the best kind: no one is too young to gain pleasure from the company of horses.

your familiar sure-footed horse which knows its own way home in the twilight.

In our modern world where everything happens at the touch of a button – where the oven cleans itself and the washing-machine does all our rinsing and drying – more and more of us are becoming obscurely aware that we're missing out on something. We can make up this deficit, at least in part, by becoming closely involved with horses. They will enrich our lives in many ways, not least because, by discovering the harmony that can exist between human being and animal, we may also discover the inner harmony that can exist inside us. After all, human beings don't function at the touch of a button and, while this makes them in many senses more difficult to 'operate', it also means that there is a deep and truly rewarding pleasure to be gained from discovering our own inner unity. We can achieve superficial, skin-deep happiness out of a lack of *un*happiness, such as when we lie out in the sun with a cold drink at our elbow, but this is very different from *true* happiness, which must come from within. One way of tapping that great well of pleasure which we all have is through our

adventures with the horse.

Nowhere has the author seen this more graphically in action than in an encounter she once had in California with a young woman and her horse. The horse was a magnificent pale-bronze stallion – a Palomino right out of the picture books, shining like a freshly struck gold coin, with a long, snowy-white mane. Its owner was playing with it in the corral. One moment it would be nuzzling her . . . the next it would be racing away to lie down on the ground and roll around, shaking its foaming white mane and every so often softly whinnying or emitting a shrill squeal to express its sheer, primitive enjoyment of life. It was the sort of scene which you don't really believe exists until you come across it for yourself.

The young woman explained her relationship with her horse, and in so doing encapsulated the sort of self-discovery through horses that was described above:

> Whenever I have some free time, which isn't very often, I like to come down here. Sometimes I just sit at the edge of the corral or on the paddock gate and watch him as he looks across at the mares, as he calls, as he stamps his hooves impatiently, as he gets mad if one of the geldings comes too close to him. Sometimes he runs up to me of his own accord; sometimes I call out to him and jump down onto the sand and crack my whip at him. I'm not trying to teach him or anything; we're just playing. You learn to react to what he's doing – and it's wonderfully relaxing, you just don't think about yourself. And when I go out riding on him or one of my other horses, I know them so much better from having watched them. We're so terribly surrounded by the technological aspects of life. With my horses I want to learn *harmony*, to get outside myself, to concentrate on something else which has its own individual laws of life.

The stallion shouted loudly and clearly.

> Can you hear? A mare has gone up to his rival and he just can't stand it. When I'm in the kitchen and hear him I know exactly what's happening outside. Horses have so many different ways of expressing themselves. Sometimes he whinnies softly and makes a sort of low hum, but other times he squeals like a pig. Or early in the morning he can wake up everything and everybody with a great triumphant clarion call – and all the other horses

Tyrolean farmers still rely on their Haflinger ponies for transport and a host of other tasks.

answer him back from their meadows and stables. And when I arrive with a handful of molasses for him he gives me a sort of happy anticipatory snort. He's talking to me.

Of course, you can't experience this richness of partnership with animals if your horse spends 23 hours of every day shut up in its stable and forgotten about. The only way the partnership can really flourish is if you spend a lot of time together. We're lucky, in this modern day and age, that many of us do have enough leisure time and financial resources to be able to include horses in our daily lives – as a sort of spiritual

Icelandic boys leading their pony through the valley almost as if it were a big dog.

vaccination against the technological virus.

That this isn't just the type of over-sentimentalism of which townspeople are so often accused, a nostalgia for a dream-like past that never actually existed, was borne out by another interview which the author conducted, this time with a modern and very businesslike farmer. Modern and businesslike he might be, but he still owned a horse. When asked about this his immediate response was: 'Ah – yes. Well. There are still a few things for it to do. Light work, and so on.' As soon as he'd said the words he realized that they weren't really true, and added:

'To tell you the truth, I suppose I *don't* really need it. Even the lighter work could be done just as easily with the tractor. Still, you need something you can be affectionate with. I can't call the tractor from the gate in the evenings. It doesn't

Ponies are incredibly sure-footed, so it's best to let them find their own way along when the going is bad.

come over to me like my Max, and I can't give it a lump of sugar. But Max – well, he's always waiting for me and the sugar . . .'

Learning to Ride

Some people are lucky enough never really to have to think about learning to ride: it just happens. They are the fortunate ones who have grown up with horses, in whose lives, ever since they can remember, horses have played a central part, and who have been riding on ponies ever since their legs grew long enough for them to 'climb aboard'. Most people, however, have to make a conscious decision to learn to ride, and most often this means finding a good riding school. Local directories will provide names and addresses, but there is no way of telling whether or not they are any good. One way to find out is to inquire about the qualifications of the tutors, but this is not an infallible guide. The best way of learning how good a riding school might be is by word of mouth. Local riders will be only too willing to give you their opinions, as will your favourite saddler; but, generally speaking, the best people to consult are the parents of children who have learnt or who are learning to ride. They

165

will openly tell you whether or not the instructors are sympathetic and experienced or bristly and nervous. And learning how children get along at riding school will be useful, even if you are fully grown up yourself: it doesn't matter if you are six or sixty when you first get into the saddle.

There are various items of equipment which you *must* have, and it is worth buying the best. The item of paramount importance is a hard hat. Some stables are prepared to lend hats to those taking lessons, but really you should have your own; obviously, with a child, it is worth borrowing a hat for the first few lessons in case the child suddenly loses interest – although that is unlikely to happen. You should also be prepared to invest in a good pair of boots. If you feel that riding boots are simply too expensive, at least to start with, then you should make sure that you wear a pair of lace-up shoes with heels, so that your foot cannot slip through the stirrup-iron and therefore that you can get your foot free if you have a fall. The riding school will advise you about further items – such as a crop – but there are a couple of points about dress that are worth noting. Firstly, wear well fitting trousers or stretch jeans. Secondly, if you're a woman, wear a bra, even if you don't normally: this has nothing to do with decorum, everything to do with comfort.

Most people who go to riding schools are girls between the ages of about 10 and 15. Riding is almost a secondary issue with them: what they're seeking is the close contact with horses – a favourite horse to enjoy grooming, feeding, watering, and telling their friends about. There are all sorts of psychological reasons for this, the most important of which is that the girls are using the horse as a way of 'finding themselves', of coping with the transitional years of adolescence. Many girls lose all interest in horses by about the age of 20, then come back to riding in later life.

Generally speaking (and this is very general), boys come to the sport later in life, usually when they are young men rather than boys. By the time they do so they are often much more interested in competition than in straightforward riding itself, even if the competition is just a matter of showing off. This is perhaps why competitive riding is dominated by men at the moment, although another important reason is that after marriage women tend to be left with the children while their husbands feel free to carry on their sport.

Riding school is only a stage in one's riding career, of course. Ideally, the next step is to own a horse for oneself, although most of us cannot afford that. However, there are various ways in which you can arrange to have easy access to horses and, if you are lucky, exclusive access to a favourite one.

The Right Horse for the Right Rider

On the European mainland it used to be that horses used for riding were big, heavy animals, but this has changed in the last few decades. Within a comparatively short space of time the accent has shifted to medium-sized horses, brought in from all parts of the world; at the same time, some of Europe's own native horses or specialist breeds began to draw attention to themselves. Soon people were riding Lipizzaners from Yugoslavia, Fjord Horses from Norway and Denmark, Welsh Ponies, Cobs and New Forest Ponies from England, Connemaras from Ireland, Iceland Ponies, the wild horses of the Camargue . . . and so on. Horses from behind the Iron Curtain became popular in Western Europe, as did the Haflinger from Austria, the Quarter-horse from the United States, and the Paso Fino from Latin America. The number of breeds which became established in Western Europe within a very few years is astonishing, and most of them are now permanent fixtures.

Right from the start these newcomers were fascinatingly different from their oh-so-civilized predecessors: they were shaggy in winter, with long and often matted hair and tousled manes, and shining clean in the summer, washed by the rain and dried by the wind. They were real back-to-nature specimens. People who had become used to the uniformly short-haired breeds, housed in the warmth of stables for much of the year, were astonished at the seasonal changes of the 'new' horses. Moreover, the newcomers bred quickly; it seemed that you could hardly turn your back without a couple of new foals appearing in the paddock.

Throughout continental Europe riding began to be seen in a different light. With the 'new' horses came ideas about different styles of riding: people looked at the ways in which other countries rode, and tried to imitate them. The principles of horse-care changed as well. People discovered that it was by no means just ponies that needed to be kept 'wild', but that all breeds of horses are healthier and happier if kept close to nature in an open stable; if they are allowed to grow a coat in winter; if they can experience the changing temperatures of different seasons and the difference between night and day. Millions of years of evolution had prepared horses for climatic extremes, so it was hardly to be wondered at that the animals had difficulty accommodating themselves to the constant warmth and generous year-round feeding of the stables.

For many Europeans a life with horses developed into a partnership which was far more satisfying than ever just a weekly ride around a track could hope to be. True, it needed more work – looking after one's own horses, making stables

Once they have found that it's safe and not too deep, ponies really enjoy trotting in water.

for them, fencing off fields, grooming them, keeping them healthy, tending the sick ones, and so on – but it all seemed to be worthwhile. Some people moved to the outskirts of town or to villages beyond so they could keep an eye on their horses and spend their leisure time with them. It was one of the most profound effects of the backlash against technology.

Countless thousands of horses have entered family lives in Western Europe since the 1940s, although this figure is dwarfed by the millions which have done the same in the United States since the 1920s. And people with large families have discovered that it is not nearly so much hard work looking after a horse as they thought it would be: when children love horses they soon develop a lasting sense of duty towards them and do all the various jobs of looking after them with a will. In fact, if your children don't develop this sense, and you haven't the time to look after the horse properly yourself, you should be kind to the horse and sell it to a better home. But almost

always the children will be only too eager to take charge. One German mother recalled:

> They took it in turns to lead them to the field, brought them to feed in the trough, cleaned the paddock and stable, rode to the farrier and greatly looked forward to the weekends we all spent together in the fresh air, to the holidays high in the mountains when we all climbed over the scree high above the tree-line. We never had any problems over the children growing up. They had an important, meaningful task to carry out, and all of us shared the joys and problems of these fascinating 'members of the family'.

For this mother at least, the whole set-up was ideal: the children looked after the horses, and the horses in a way looked after the children, helping them to avoid most of the difficult problems involved with adolescence.

Riding used to be an almost prohibitively expensive activity in Western Europe, and in days gone by a family was lucky if a single member could afford to indulge in the hobby. This has now changed, and riding has become a fulfilling habit for entire families. Because it has now gradually come to be realized that the medium-sized horses are strong, willing and of good temperament, more and more adults are today riding horses up to 15 hands high – something new to continental Europe, even if common in other parts of the world. Living with the family, loved by young and old, the horses grow even closer to us than we could ever have dreamed possible. They tolerate the clumsily gentle touch of the smaller children, acknowledge the friendship of boisterous boys and girls, and give adults hours of relaxation in the form of refreshing rides through the countryside. The mother quoted above was right when she described the horses as 'members of the family'.

In the United Kingdom and the United States the change hasn't been nearly so dramatic, because people in those countries have had a much longer tradition of family riding. In the United States, in particular, as standards of living have risen over the last few decades more and more people from the cities have discovered that it is possible to afford the upkeep of horses for the family. Many people have the opportunity to discover the additional self-fulfilment in life which contact with horses can bring. In the United Kingdom horse-ownership is considerably less widespread than in either continental Europe or North America, not only for reasons of expense but also because there is so much less by way of available pasture-land. Nonetheless, thanks to the fact that so many more people now have extra disposable income with which to indulge their hobbies (at the same time as, paradoxically, so many people have had to learn to make do with less), riding is gently on the increase. In addition, people are finding more and more ways of being able to concentrate their attentions on a particular, favourite horse, rather than just whatever the riding school chooses to lend them this week.

The matter of having a favourite horse is an

A competitor at the European Championships using the rack, a swift and comfortable gait lost for centuries in Europe.

A Thoroughbred that has been taught to rack in the way that its ancestors did naturally centuries ago.

important one. If you are lucky enough to be able to afford to buy a horse, there are a number of practical things which you should do – have an expert assess the horse for you, call in the veterinary surgeon to check it out, and so on. Numerous horse manuals will tell you all the theoretical details. But there is one thing everyone will tell you to look for when thinking of buying a horse, and that is whether you get on with it. If you *like* the horse, and if it appears to like you, then many of your possible problems will be solved before they even occur. This is particularly important if you're planning to buy a horse for your children: all their protestations that they will take full charge of care and maintenance will soon be forgotten if they just don't *like* the horse you've bought them. That would be cruel to

the horse and not very fair to the children, so try to have the horse on trial so that you can get to know it before you decide whether or not to buy it. Afterwards is too late.

Gaits

Forty years ago, when Icelandic horses first returned to the lands their ancestors had left thousands of years before, they brought with them, as well as different ideas about the way a horse should look, surprises in terms of the gaits with which a horse should move. Western Europeans recognized walking, trotting, cantering and galloping as the 'natural' gaits of a horse, so it was something of a revelation to find horses which paced and racked. The pace has already been described in terms of the American Standardbred

Overleaf, one of the great pleasures of riding is that it brings you close to nature in surroundings such as these.

(page 80): the horse moves its legs in pairs, the pairs consisting of the two legs on the same side of the body, and does so in two-step time: 1-2-1-2-1-2. The pace is a gait indigenous to many of the world's breeds, where it replaces or complements the trot as a way of getting about. But the rack?

Familiar in North America for a long time, the rack was new to Europe and in the United Kingdom is still never seen. It came as something of a surprise to European riders. At first they couldn't understand how it was that, as the horse's pace increased, the back did not arch up slightly – as in trotting – but rolled gently downwards under the horse's own bodyweight. Riders could hear the hooves tapping out a four-step beat – 1-2-3-4-1-2-3-4 – but they couldn't work out exactly how the horse did it. In the end they had to call upon all the sophisticated assistance of modern technology, in the form of slow-motion cameras and so on, to discover that what the horse was doing was moving in a sort of broken pace where, instead of the two legs on the same

It's fun to splash and feel the sunshine and the water on your bare skin in the summer.

A pure-bred Palomino: there's no need to ride to enjoy the sheer beauty of its movement, colour and shape.

side stepping simultaneously, they were moving just after one another. As soon as this was realized racking became a recognized gait, and nowadays there are specialized competitions involving it – just as there have been for ages in Iceland and North America.

But the amusing thing was that, as soon as people realized the rack existed, they found that horses had been using it since time immemorial. There it was, perfectly clear, on medieval woodcuts showing people riding; and look, there it was in all the classic writings on horsemanship right up until about the seventeenth century. In medieval German writings you can find abundant mention of a gait known as the *Zelt* – and ladies' horses during the Middle Ages were often called *Zelters*. People had always assumed that what was meant by the *Zelt* was the amble, but now it seemed self-evident that the word *Zelt* was simply the Germanic form of the Icelandic word

tölt, meaning 'rack'. Moreover, literary researches into medieval accounts showed that the *Zelter* hadn't been just a ladies' horse at all, but was the comfortable riding horse used by everyone. The knights of the Middle Ages, for example, used to ride to the wars on *Zelters*, changing over to their trotting battle steeds, which had been brought along by their pages, for the combat itself.

How had the rack come to be forgotten in Western Europe? In the courtly form of riding which came to dominate the scene in later centuries the important yardstick was Haute École (see pages 120–23), which gave birth to dressage and so led to the general misconception that there was no other form of riding. The cavalry traditions involved having horses moving together in close formation, which meant that you needed horses which could trot exactly together; and with the development of the Thoroughbred for racing the tempo of all riding suddenly became faster. This trend towards more rapid movement was reinforced not just on the racecourse or in the hunt: during the seventeenth and eighteenth centuries Europe's road networks vastly im-

proved and the well sprung carriage came into its own. Travellers no longer needed to cope with the discomforts of riding on a horse that was trotting or galloping at speed because they could relax into lush upholstery instead. The gentle, slow movement of the rack just disappeared, both from the roads and from people's memories.

In other countries this did not occur. The settlers who emigrated from Western Europe in the sixteenth and seventeenth centuries to the Americas and to the southern hemisphere didn't take the idea of courtly riding with them, and it would be two centuries or more before they built up good road networks. What they did take with them, however, were the best breeds of horses – *comfortable* horses – which they still breed expertly today. During the American Civil War, for example, the Southern forces found it an object of derision that their more 'civilized' Northern counterparts bobbed up and down so unnaturally in the saddle. Nowadays, in the southern states of Kentucky, Tennessee and Missouri they still breed large, elegant fiery horses with a wonderfully comfortable gait; prime examples are the Tennessee Walking Horse and the five-gaited American Saddle Horse. These were horses for everyday use, not just for display, and their rack-related gaits were and still are especially sought.

The rack is found, under various different names, all over the world. In Mongolia a horse with a trained racking gait is three times as valuable as one which can only trot; and a natural

Above, *the leading pony knows the way so well that he doesn't even need a bridle.*

racker which can maintain this gait for hours on end is worth eight times as much. In Russia the Turkish Armenians kept the rack (*perestrup*) alive. In fact, there was hardly a country in the world that didn't have a selection of racking horses except in Western Europe, where they were confined to the seclusion of Iceland and the Spanish Basque country.

Because the gait is such a natural one, you don't really have to look for a horse specially trained in racking: most horses will do it if *you* are the one to learn to make the change. Racing trotters soon become ideal horses for leisure riding if you give them a longer rein. In fact, the gait to which they have been trained is both unnatural and uncomfortable for them. Their build is not really suited to it: if the nose is held down, the long back stretches and this is painful; but if the nose is left to do what the horse wants it to do, the back will hollow slightly and the horse will move in a superb rack or comfortable canter.

Racing trotters, ridden in this way, are excellent horses for leisure-time riding. They don't need to be pampered in any way: they can spend their time outdoors all year round so long as they have constant access to an open stable. Their hair grows to a woolly fur, and they lose the highly strung temperament of the average racing horse, developing instead (or, rather, rediscovering) a charming good nature which horse-lovers everywhere eulogize. These admirable horses don't have to be written off as soon as their racing careers are over. Far from it: they have many useful years ahead of them during which they can happily fulfil the role of family friend.

The 'rediscovery' of the rack on the European mainland has created something of a revolution in leisure riding there. Is it, perhaps, too much to hope that in the near future the same sort of thing will come about in Britain, which is now almost alone in the world in not recognizing the rack as the easy, natural and – for rider and horse alike – delightfully comfortable gait which it is?

Holidays with Horses
There are all sorts of options open to people who would like to spend their holidays with horses. In every country there is a great diversity of riding holidays available, based on riding schools, farms, and so on; for children there are summer camps with ponies and horses. These are especially well organized in the United States, Holland and Britain, and for many children represent their first experience of horses. But riding isn't the only way. Many city-dwellers can get away from it all by spending a fortnight rambling in a horse-drawn caravan through the quiet parts of Ireland, Holland or France: as a faithful carthorse pulls them ploddingly along in their temporary home, complete with beds and a kitchen, they can have all the joys of moving *slowly* along paths and small country byroads, miles from anywhere, enjoying the flowers by the roadside and the clouds in the sky, and deliciously losing all track of time.

Below, *tourists enjoy a ride in typical Hungarian style by the side of the water in Hortobagy Puszta.*

Overleaf, *Hungarian horses of the Shagya breed, created on Arab stock and now bred in the USA.*

It is this slowness which makes the modern riding holiday so popular: for a couple of weeks in the year you don't have to rush the whole time, but can take things easy. People have rediscovered the immense satisfaction they can get from long horseback treks, enjoying new parts of the countryside that they've never seen before, staying in different places every night, some of which can be an adventure in themselves, finding their way through new surroundings, taking unexpected detours when something goes wrong with the navigation, suddenly coming across a wide stretch of path that's just begging to be galloped along, picking their way with a pounding heart along a narrow mountainside track above the blue waters of a lake, seemingly miles below. . . And then, at nights, there are the joys of camping with the horses whinnying gently in the dusk.

This form of mounted tourism is greatly on the increase in Europe among both owners and hirers of horses. Belgium and Luxembourg have a fantastic network of bridle-paths, complete with stables which you can hire for the night and inns where you can get accommodation for yourself. In France there are now paths marked out all through the Massif Central, from the Pyrenees to the Dutch border and from Brest to Provence. Spain offers a wide range of riding routes through the wildly beautiful sierras and along the southern coast; in all the Eastern-bloc countries there are stud-farms and riding stables which welcome visitors; Italy has opened up the Abruzzi, its south-central region between the Apennines and the Adriatic, to riders; Morocco offers ten-day tours through the Atlas Mountains; and in the United Kingdom and Eire trekking has for decades been the favourite pastime of thousands, who flee from the bustle of the cities to find peace and quiet in the mountains of Scotland or in the wild, beautiful country of Exmoor and Dartmoor in southwestern England. In many countries

Below, *both pony and rider need a good head for heights as they make their way along this ledge.*

Right, *visitors to Canada riding the trail – a popular form of holiday for people from all over the world.*

whole industries have sprung up around trekking holidays: there are new trekking saddles, leather accessories, saddlebags and tents, as well as build-it-yourself sheds and stabling in which horse-owners can keep their animals when they are not out riding them. Anyone can now find, somewhere, the holiday with horses to suit both them and their pocket.

But it would be wrong to think that this phenomenon is confined in any way to Europe. In Canada, day- and week-long trail rides are popular, not only with North Americans but also among visiting Europeans, some of whom come over specially. You take your supplies with you on pack-horses, and you can camp or stay in log cabins in the huge National Parks. Moving along slowly in the company of a handful of other riders you begin to feel as if there's no one else in the world. The only sounds are the sounds of nature, carrying on as if you weren't there. You get the impression that you are the first human being ever to pass that way.

From the north of the Americas to the south of Africa: to Lesotho, the mountainous country of the 'African Indians' (see page 53). Here you can ride across the breathtakingly beautiful plateaux, thousands of feet above sea-level, while all around you the mountains stretch even higher, seeming almost to touch the sky. This is the ultimate in natural beauty, with not a trace of humanity to be seen anywhere. Unless, that is, you want there to be – because riding here can also mean getting to know new people, new riders. Tiny, narrow paths, barely discernible, weave their way through Lesotho's rough mountain landscape. These are the paths that have been etched out by the whites: Lesotho's inhabitants, the Basuto, use them only when they feel like it, generally preferring just to follow their noses in a dead straight line, whatever the natural obstacles they have to cross. This can be rather alarming if you have hired a Basuto to act as your guide; but these exquisite horsemen have a single response which silences you should you ever start to remonstrate with them about all the dangers through which they have cheerfully led you. Have you never considered that a horse has four legs, rather than two, and so is only half as likely to slip? This may not be strictly logical, but what the Basuto is getting at is that your mount will hardly ever be in any difficulties, no matter what the terrain underfoot, if there exists between it and you that deep trust and sense of partnership which used to be common in the relationship between human beings and their animal friends.

Perhaps nowhere else in the world except in Mongolia – where the opportunities for riding holidays are rather limited! – can you get this same feeling of travelling back in time to enjoy the relationship with horses that our primitive ancestors experienced. In the United States, however, you can holiday among people who share an equally valid partnership with their horses, the cowboys. You have to pick and choose, of course – there are dude ranches and dude ranches – but if you are lucky you will find yourself in the company of quiet, gentle men and their equally quiet, relaxed horses. Men and horses work together and play together; they share their lives with each other. As you learn how to use your horse the same way that the cowboys use theirs in their everyday work, you will learn something else that is of inestimable value in all walks of life: that in order to do something real and meaningful you have to find out how sometimes to 'do nothing'. You will learn that your citified hurrying and scurrying, your constant urge to be *busy*, are just not compatible with the laws of nature – as exemplified by your patient mount.

If this is the kind of self-discovery you want from your holiday with horses, then it is not too difficult to organize. In many parts of the United States there are long-established dude (or tenderfoot) ranches where you can go for a few days or weeks to learn as much about ranch life as is good for you. You will find yourself introduced to the cowboy way of life by real cowboys – not dressed-up imitations – who know their work and take it seriously. Many of the dude ranches are big enough to take 100 or 150 guests at a time, with a horse for each. Sorted into easily manageable groups, townspeople learn how to collect horses from the pastures, to bridle and saddle them, to ride them properly, in the cowboy manner, and then follow experienced leaders out into the great open country to explore the natural beauties to be found there. They are given a gentle, trustworthy horse to ride; sit in a solid, deep Western-style saddle; go on long pack-trips, spending the nights in tents with only the stars above. They ride on narrow paths through the mountains, look down on distant lakes and ravines, squint up at the mountaintops, gaze all around at a panorama of endless plains . . . and all the time their sturdy companion is their horse, which takes them on to their destination for the night, asking only to be stripped of its saddle, fed, watered and tethered as a reward.

This is all a far cry from the kind of holiday with horses to be enjoyed on a farm in Britain.

Above, the pony on the left has no intention of running away, but eats contentedly after its long climb.

Below, cowboys in the USA enjoying a few moments' relaxation before setting off on their long ride home.

Nevertheless, the pleasures are rather similar. The British Isles cannot perhaps afford the dramatic scenery of Lesotho or the sense of space to be felt when riding in the plains of North America, but you can still experience the same deep appreciation of and closeness to nature, seeing its beauties on the small rather than the vast scale. Also, you can discover the same partnership of trust not only with horses but also with the other animals on the farm. As well as riding the horses, you get the opportunity to feed and tend them, to help nurse any sick ones there might be, to become really involved in the magic of the horse. The people you meet on the farm are also rewarding: you will be surprised at the contrast between those people and many of your acquaintances of the city. (That's if you're lucky, of course – but then that's true of any type of holiday.) Moreover, if you choose carefully, this type of holiday need not necessarily be too dear.

The standards of riding holidays and the horses used on them in the British Isles are generally high, and you can ride virtually anywhere, depending upon the terrain and upon private-property restrictions. Scotland is perfectly suited to trail-riding (often called post-trekking) as well as to straightforward pony-trekking. There is little in the way of road-work involved. Most of it is across the wild hillside: the horses used are generally tough Highland ponies. There are many centres which have received the approval of the Scottish Sports Council, and lists of these are available from the Scottish Tourist Board.

In recent years one of the biggest booms in trekking has been in Wales; a list of suitable centres has been produced by the Pony Trekking Society of Wales. In northern England there is fine riding in Cumbria, Northumbria and Yorkshire, although here it is rather difficult to find suitable centres: for the best of reasons, however – these regions are as yet uncommercialized. Further south, in the warmer English West Country, there is unlimited riding country among the high tors and the wild moors of Exmoor and Dartmoor, as well as in the generally gentler countryside of the New Forest, with its wild ponies and deer, and the South Downs Way in Sussex. If you want a holiday with horses in the United Kingdom you will find the handbooks of the British Horse Society and of the Association of British Riding Schools invaluable, as well as the regional guides already mentioned.

For a holiday that is completely different, though, you could travel to Russia and find out what it's like to travel in a troika. Near Moscow, in Ostankino Park, which covers more than 2500 acres (1000 ha), the typical Russian triple-span teams of horses are harnessed up for the benefit of native and foreign tourists. In summer they pull four-wheeled coaches, in winter fabulous brightly painted sleighs. The drivers and passengers are wrapped up in heavy fur coats to keep out the winter chill and as the bells on the trappings ring out across the snow it will all change your perception of winter completely. You will never forget flying across the endless snowfields, through the wide rides of the park or out across the open countryside.

Travelling slowly in the bitter cold of the Russian winter is not practicable: the horses would soon freeze up. The driver therefore ensures that they keep up at least a steady trot, and preferably will let them run fast. One peculiarity of troika-driving is that, while the centre horse of the three should always be trotting, the outer two should be moving at the canter. Moreover, the centre horse is running between a pair of shafts, just like a single-yoked horse, while both outside horses are attached to the sleigh by light leather traces and to the centre horse by leather straps. In fact, it is the centre horse which is the one doing all the pulling; the other two merely assist if the load is too heavy or the terrain becomes difficult. The *duga*, the wooden yoke on the centre horse of the troika, is used also for single-yoked horses by the people of the Baltic countries – Latvia, Lithuania and Poland. It is wide and edged with iron, or brightly painted, and has the effect of keeping the shafts together.

The way in which the troika is driven is like nothing that has been mentioned before. The driver has one pair of reins for each horse, and he winds these around both hands, driving with his arms outstretched. The outside reins are usually kept short, so that they pull the horses' heads outwards, thereby keeping them at the correct gallop. Only when the two side horses have to take a part in pulling the sleigh does the driver loosen their reins. He does not use a whip; it would be too difficult to handle, because both his hands are fully occupied with the reins.

As well as the troika there is also a four-span coach called a *tatsjanka*. Here there are two middle horses, harnessed up in the same way as a pair pulling one of the two-span coaches more familiar to Western European eyes, with two linked horses on the outsides, just as with the troika.

If you visit Moscow in winter you should be lucky enough to see one of the troika races held there on the racecourse. Watching the sleighs battle for position is a thrilling experience – but perhaps not quite of the same order as riding in one of the sleighs yourself!

Russian horses resting after the exertion of pulling the troika in Moscow. A ride in a troika is thrilling, but if you visit Moscow you may have to settle for watching the troika races instead.

Above, in the Russian winter it is essential to travel fast to counter the effects of the cold. In troika-driving the central horse maintains a steady trot while the outside two canter. The horse in the centre runs between a pair of shafts while the outer ones are attached to the sleigh by traces and to the central horse by straps.

Below, a ride in a troika is an experience you will never forget. In troika-driving it is the central horse that does the main work: the others help when the load is exceptionally heavy or the going particularly difficult. The duga, the decorated wooden yoke on the central horse, is used also all through the Baltic countries for single-yoke horses.

AT THE CIRCUS

Any exploration of the world of the horse would be incomplete without a trip to the circus . . .

On 29th January, 1914, as a highlight of the winter season, a riding banquet took place in the monumental stone building of the Circus Sarasani in Dresden. Among the luminaries assembled in the audience were the King of Saxony and three other princes. The most brilliant equestrian achievement was the demonstration of Haute École by an uhlan (lancers) officer. Also there was a chief sergeant of the royal stables performing free dressage; and a lieutenant gave a breathtaking display of bareback riding. The court was thrilled and enchanted by the beauty of the horses and the skill and dare-devilry of their riders. And then, only a few months later, this scene and others like it were consigned to the half-forgotten recesses of history as the blood and slaughter of World War I brutally terminated the era of courtly elegance.

But the circus itself survived, and any of us can go to see it.

The word 'circus' comes from Latin and beyond that from the Greek *kirkos*, meaning 'ring'. The ring in question is the focus of the whole circus, and is a comparatively recent invention. It all began in 1769 when an ex-cavalry Sergeant-Major named Philip Astley, who made a living out of giving demonstrations of horsemanship, roped off a ring because he found that it was easier to stand on the back of his horse if it were cantering around in a circle. He introduced other innovations to these displays of horsemanship, including the supplementation of his trick-riding act with tumblers, jesters and, later, wild animals. He is rightly acclaimed as the founder of the modern circus, although the word itself, in today's sense, was first used by one of his rivals, Charles Hynes.

Nowadays the circus ring has internationally agreed dimensions, all of which are defined in terms of horses. It has a radius of 6·5 m (21 ft 4 in) and the surrounding low barrier is 50 cm (20 in) high and 35 cm (14 in) wide. The radius has settled at this dimension because it has been found to be just right for horses to gallop around in a circle of this size: any smaller and their gallop would be restricted and broken; any larger and they would have difficulty in staying exactly the same distance from each other at all times, a matter of some importance when they are providing a moving foundation for juggling acts and so forth. Likewise it has been found to be the ideal size for horses to perform free dressage. Here the animals are instructed by the trainer through the use of a long baton called a *chambrière*. Experience has shown that the optimal length of the *chambrière* is 5·5 m (18 ft): any longer and it is unmanageable; any shorter and the trainer has to run around too much. 5·5 m is in fact the radius of the ring less the trainer's arm-length.

The trainer uses the *chambrière* constantly. A gentle touch with it and the horses change pace or direction, kneel down, or rear up on their hind-legs. He uses it to talk to his equine charges as clearly as if they were all using the medium of the spoken word. As the experts have discovered, one of the secrets of successful dressage lies in the use of the whip just to touch the horse: it is controlled to perfection, and never on any account allowed to degenerate into an instrument of pain.

The barrier, as we have said, is also sized with regard to its use by the horses. It has to be just the right height for the horse to stand on it with its forelegs and yet still be able to use its hindlegs unhindered in the ring. In addition, it must be wide enough for a skilful horse to trot along it without falling off. The ground inside the ring is tailored for equestrian performances, too. It is covered with sawdust on top of sand, so that the horses are given a bouncing gait. Nearer to the barrier it is somewhat raised to stop the horses from accidentally kicking the wooden edge.

Horses have been central to the circus ever since Astley's day. Originally the star performers were ex-cavalry officers like Astley himself; but

Left, the horses in the Swiss National Circus are trained to perfection by succeeding generations of the Knie family. Here Fredy Knie Jr and his wife Mary-José perform an elegant pas de deux *with perfect rhythm and style, upholding the high standards always maintained by the family.*

Below, the barrier around the ring is specially constructed to provide a suitable platform for the liberty horses.

Overleaf, these Lipizzaner stallions rising majestically as if from the waves exemplify all the magic of the circus.

soon there were specialist horsemen (and, very significantly, horsewomen) who were trained or who trained themselves specifically for the circus-ring. The most spectacular performances were those of free dressage, in which unridden horses carried out movements and tricks in response to nothing more than verbal instructions, hand signals, or light touches with the *chambrière*. The horses pretended to be dead, jumped through rings of fire, reared up, turned, marched and danced in time to music, doing all of these things either singly or in groups of up to 30 horses. Thus they were continuing a tradition stretching right back to long before the modern circus began, all the way to the great circuses of the Roman emperors, when equestrian displays played their part among the gorier demonstrations of the gladiators, the lions and the Christians.

It was in the middle of the nineteenth century that the golden age of circus Haute École began, and the riders of this era could teach even the cavalry officers a thing or two. Performers like the Father and Daughter Renz, Albert Schumann, Busch and countless others fascinated a highly knowledgeable audience. They combined genius in horsemanship with the imaginative flair to bring other people's fantasies to life. Some of the spectacles created in those days are still performed today, such as the 'Black Horse Jumper' in which six black horses jump a wall in the middle of the ring in twos, threes, fours or all together, backwards and forwards at astonishing speed.

The horses shown in these pages are from the Swiss National Circus, which was founded over 50 years ago. Under the tutelage of six generations of the Knie family, these horses have shown themselves capable of enacting your dreams. As you sit in the darkness of the audience, all your attention focused on the brilliantly illuminated ring and the horses performing in it, you will be convinced as perhaps nowhere else that you are in the presence of magic.

Acknowledgements

The photographs in this book are by: Colorsport (pp 110, 112); Werner Ernst (p 119); Kit Houghton (pp 77, 111, 113, 114, 115, 116, 117, 120, 124, 157); Ewald Isenbügel (pp 17, 50, 155, 162, 164, 168, 170/71, 178, 181 bottom); Octopus Books Ltd (pp 1, 68); Karl Schütz (p 163); Dirk Schwager (pp 9, 57, 129, 133, 148, 149); Hans W. Silvester (pp 14, 20); H. Sting (p 106); Tony Stone (Endpapers, pp 2/3); ZEFA (pp 6/7). The photographs on pp 13, 25, 54, 63, 64, 65, 66 top l, 66 top r, 66 bottom l, 67 top l, 67 top r, 95, 96/7, 98, 99, 142/3, 144 top, 144 bottom l, 144 bottom r, 145, 147 top, 147 bottom, 150, 165, 167, 169, 173, 174, 175, 176/7, 181 top, are by the author, while the remainder are by Elisabeth Weiland.

Index

Page numbers in *italics* refer to relevant captions.